HISTORY: MEANING AND METHOD

HISTORY: MEANING AND METHOD

Revised Edition

DONALD V. GAWRONSKI
Florissant Valley Community College

Consulting Editor
RUSSEL B. NYE
Michigan State University

SCOTT, FORESMAN AND COMPANY

Library of Congress Catalog Card No. 74–79690

FOREWORD

Historians, it is said, are not completely confident that they can define precisely what history is. This is not a reflection on historians; rather, it means simply that history is as complex, variable, and puzzling as the people whose lives and acts it records. Like literature, philosophy, and the arts, history is a way of looking at human experience—at the lives of the individuals who are its parts and at the life of the society which is the sum. What is history's importance to the United States in the later twentieth century? What does it have to say of value to a world taut with tensions and shadowed by doubt?

First, it must be understood that history is a response to the eternal desire of man to know about himself and others. For this reason it is fundamentally a humane study, emphasizing the importance of people, their individual choices, the values they hold, and the angles of vision by which they have looked at themselves and the world. This pervading interest in humanity is the vital link between history and other humanistic disciplines with which it shares tools and objectives. But because history deals primarily with man in *time*, it offers a way of looking at human experience that the other humanistic disciplines do not: History brings depth to the study of man, giving it a past perspective and a sense of the inevitability of change. Because history deals with the flow of things, it shows that nothing stands still, that experience is dynamic and continuous; it lets us know that while what is happening now is important, men have had problems before and have survived them. One of history's most valuable contributions to its reader and writer is that it puts the present in its proper place.

Second, history is concerned with societies as well as with individuals. Like social scientists, historians are interested in how—and hopefully, why—men have acted together as social beings. Because of its link with the social sciences, history uses the same hypotheses and findings to observe how men have developed their institutions, what they have used them for, and how they have acted within the political, social, and cultural frameworks by which they order their lives. The purpose of the historian, as Marcel Proust once defined that of the novelist, is "to rediscover, to grasp again and lay before us, that reality from which we have been so far removed by time . . . ," that is, to recapture the reasons which lie beneath action by recovering the experience.

Since history is interested in *causes*, it enlarges and clarifies our comprehension of the social process; it tries to provide a more disciplined view of some of the social problems that beset us. There is more than a little truth to Santayana's famous observation that "those who do not know history are doomed to repeat it," for to know how society has operated in the past may serve to remind us of the possibilities and alternatives inherent in the present. History cannot tell the present exactly what to do, but it may help it to avoid making the same mistakes over again. Today's society can distill something out of the past that may be useful for its guidance, for history has a kind of built-in early warning system for those who know how to listen to it.

Third, history emphasizes the uniqueness of man's experience, both individual and collective. As we read history, we begin to recognize that life is idiosyncratic and variable and that each piece of it has its own integrity. However attractive the parallels between past and present may be, we soon learn that the past is not really repetitive, that history never does quite repeat itself. History warns us that we cannot trust reiteration, that we cannot say that what worked once, or failed once, will do so again. It serves as a corrective to too much self-confidence and too-easy answers, reminding us that we are very, very human. George Kennan, who turned to the study of history (and won a Pulitzer Prize in it) after a distinguished diplomatic career, once pointed out that in an era of spectacular scientific and technological change, when the planets themselves seem accessible to man, "he needs to be reminded of the nature of the species he belongs to, of the limitations that rest upon him, of the essential elements, both tragic and hopeful, of his own condition. It is these reminders that history, and history alone, can give."

Fourth, while all the humanities have the duty of conserving, transmitting, and interpreting experience, history has the special obligation to recall, reassess, and reinterpret the past, bringing it to bear on the present and translating it into a form each new generation can use. Historians deal, of course, in facts with an actual past, tied to a particular plane of reality and fixed immovably by the iron law of the documented date. But they deal not only in fact but in *feel*; they try to infuse facts with insights into the quality, tempo, temper, and meaning of the life in which they are rooted. Facts, despite the saying, do not speak for themselves; they say something only when chosen, arranged, and interpreted. Albert Bushnell Hart remarked a half-century ago, "Facts as facts are no more history than recruits arrayed in battalions are an army."

More than literature, philosophy, or the arts, history selects and judges. It sifts the whole of man's culture again and again, finding new relevance in some segment of experience an earlier generation discarded, putting away for posterity something which for the moment has lost its usefulness but to which some future generation will give new meaning. What the historian must do, to use Samuel Eliot Morison's words, is "to relate the past *creatively* to the present." The purpose of the historian, then, is not merely to locate and understand the facts of human experience, but to transcend them by giving them values that are stimulating, suggestive, and newly pertinent to his own time. That is why history is not only written but rewritten. It is what Emerson meant when in 1851 he wrote enigmatically in his journal, "History is vanishing allegory."

RUSSEL B. NYE

Most students encounter some difficulties upon entering their first college classes. Basically these difficulties revolve around the transition from a rather rigid high school program to the greater freedom and more exacting demands of modern collegiate life. As a beginning student of college-level history you may experience these difficulties, but you may also encounter two other problems that are brought on by the nature of history courses. One of these problems is how you are going to become sufficiently interested in a survey history course so as to want to master the subject matter, some of which you have already studied several times in your earlier educational career. The other problem is how you are going to obtain the necessary tools to achieve academic success in any general history course at a level corresponding to your particular abilities.

Both of these problems stem from the fact that, to many college students at the lower division level, survey history courses appear to be nothing more than memorization courses in names, dates, and events. In the minds of many of these students (and perhaps you are one of them) history has no intrinsic value or meaning; it possesses only the highly dubious extrinsic value of being a required portion of a degree program—an ordeal which must be undergone in order to advance toward the coveted diploma.

Several reasons may be given for this negative student attitude. These reasons are offered as neither condemnation nor excuse but rather as simple observations. For one, you must remember that your instructor is faced with the perplexing problem of presenting a tremendous bulk of material within the rather cramped time period of the average survey course. As such, the history instructor is forced to follow a rather standardized ritual. He cannot cover everything that he would like to cover, nor can he afford to give every student the thorough, detailed preparation for the discipline that he would like to give. There simply is not enough class time available. Consequently many students enter their first collegiate history course with a fundamental question in their minds—a question the answer to which will oftentimes determine the success or failure of these students—"Why should we study more history?"

To the instructor the answer to this question is quite obvious; to his students the answer may not be so readily evident. The beginning student of college-level history requires a thorough orientation to the nature of history as a discipline if he is going to profit from its study. Unfortunately the instructor is placed in the position of sacrificing the presentation of some valuable historical material in order to provide a thorough orientation to the discipline, or he presents the orientation at the expense of some equally important historical fact. The material contained in this book is designed to aid both in the saving of valuable class time and in answering the fundamental question: "Why should we study more history?"

Expanding class sizes in lecture-type courses rapidly open the way to objectively scored examinations, which are either graded by selected, superior students or by machines. Essay examinations tend to be reserved primarily for upper division and graduate history students. On the objectively scored examination, emphasis is often placed on the recall of factual materials—or so it would appear. No wonder the student oftentimes regards history as a sheer memorization course, for memorizing is often his primary requirement for passing the course. He must be made aware of the significance of history if he is going to become sufficiently receptive to profit from the lessons that history teaches. If the student could acquire an understanding of what to look for and what items have the most importance in his historical studies, survey history courses could overcome to a large extent the disadvantage of size. The number of students in a class does not necessarily determine the success of individual students in that class, but special provisions must be made for the auditorium lectures that acquaint many students with their first college-level history courses in our modern educational system.

If you are going to succeed in a survey history course, you need an understanding of the purpose of your course. Obviously the intent of the survey history course is not to manufacture the expert historian— so you can breathe a sigh of relief here. The purpose of the survey history course is to serve as a general introduction to the study of man and to provide some general education—a highly confusing term in the world of modern education. The purpose of the survey history course is also to provide a solid base upon which to develop into an expert historian, if you should happen to discover that you are so inclined. Basic fact, technique, method, and what Carl Gustavson refers to as "historical mindedness" are both the goals and the justification of the lower division survey history course in the modern college curriculum.

Ideally the lower division student of history should be well equipped to write book reports and reviews, basic research papers (if the class is small enough), and reviews of articles in learned journals. But this is the ideal; it is rarely present in reality. Some students require basic instruction in these matters, for college assignments may initially appear to be quite bewildering.

There are several excellent advanced manuals on style and mechanics available, but they are designed primarily with the upper division or graduate student in mind. The lower division student does not need to know, at the present stage of his career, how to style a dissertation or handle foreign manuscript materials in his research papers.

Several years of attempting to discover a means both of generating student interest in the study of history, even if no advanced courses are contemplated, and of increasing the success probabilities of students in the survey history course have prompted this work. The intent has been to aim at the lower division student, not at the graduate student. Hence, there is absolutely no claim here to supersede or replace any of the several excellent guides to historical method, works on historiography, or studies on philosophy of history.

The material contained herein has been developed solely to serve as a general introduction to American or European survey history courses and to the discipline as a whole. It was written for the student and, in particular, for the lower division student of history. It is not designed to produce expert historians, but it can provide a solid foundation upon which the art of the historian eventually may be developed.

The book is divided into six chapters. The first deals with a definition of history as a discipline—and there are many such definitions. Chapter 2 is concerned with identifying some of the various problems that are encountered in the study of history. Chapter 3 serves as an introduction to philosophy of history and traces the development of dominant philosophies throughout history. Concerning the methodology of history, Chapter 4 contains materials on types and techniques of historical writing, suggestions for planning and organizing a term paper, and a footnoting system, both reference and content. Chapter 5 is concerned with presenting a brief treatment of the development of American historiography, while Chapter 6 attempts to serve the same purpose for medieval and modern European history.

Finally, Appendix A consists of a short bibliographical essay, followed by a bibliography containing a sampling of various types of works that the student may consult for further reading, and a rather lengthy citation of the various guides and bibliographies in the English language to which he might refer in writing a basic history research paper or in choosing a book intelligently. In a further attempt to render assistance to the beginning student, Appendix B provides a Glossary of Terms commonly used in history textbooks. And to aid in developing time perspective and in obtaining a broad picture of human developments, a time scale for the history of the earth and chronological tables of American and European history are included in Appendix C.

D.V.G.

TABLE OF CONTENTS

A DEFINITION OF HISTORY

1

Historians are not at all agreed on an exact definition of their discipline. The field is so complex that it is almost impossible to obtain
anything approaching a consensus. Consequently whenever an historian attempts a definition, he renders himself quite vulnerable. However, the definition presented below does provide a basis for classroom
discussion and argument.

In its broadest and most elementary sense, history could be defined
as a record of the past or at least part of the past. But this would not
really constitute a working definition. For one point, the definition
would be overly simplified. History is a rather complex discipline
deserving a more thorough definition. For another point, the above
definition would suggest an extremely formidable and ambitious, yet
at the same time nebulous, task for the historian because of the vast,
indefinite period of time involved. It is true that history is an ambitious discipline—but not because of the vast time period involved in
accounting for the existence of this planet.

Our introductory definition would suggest that history is concerned
with a tremendously long span of time. Actually this is not the case.
History is concerned with a very minute portion of the lifetime of the
earth. Geologists have informed us that the earth is somewhere between three and four billion years old. Man, in his most primitive
form, Zinjanthropus, is estimated to have walked the face of the earth
for something on the order of roughly 1,750,000 years.[1] History is

[1] Latest evidence suggests that Zinjanthropus may not be the oldest known
human form. See Melvin M. Payne, "Preserving the Treasures of Olduvai Gorge,"

concerned with a record of the past insofar as it applies to human beings. So at the very best, i.e., if we choose to be charitable and refer to our friend Zinjanthropus as a human being, we have narrowed our original broad definition to cover approximately 1/200th of the period during which our planet is reputed to have existed. We happily leave the rest within the realm of the geologist.[2]

Hence, our definition should read that history is a record of the *human* past. The word "record" should be emphasized also, for by emphasizing it, history can be limited to an even smaller time period than that dating from Zinjanthropus or some other primitive. Man has left written records for roughly five thousand years. And it is these five thousand years of written records that concern the discipline of history. Leaving earlier man to the study of the anthropologist and archaeologist, but not by any means ignoring their findings, the historian is actually concerned with only 1/750,000th of the lifetime of our planet, for this is the time span of "civilized" man's existence.

This is an infinitesimal period by geological standards, but it is a tremendous period by historical standards, and it provides no end of problems for the practicing historian. It also provides, however, a more exact definition of history. With this in mind, then, history is a record of the human past from the point when written records began to appear. History is the record of what we might loosely term "human civilization" as far as we are able to ascertain it.

So the historian records the facts of human existence, and this is in itself still a very formidable and ambitious task—even for such a relatively short span of time. But the historian performs two other functions as well, both of which must be included in any thorough definition of the discipline. The historian must interpret his facts in an orderly and intelligible manner. He must also attempt to discover patterns and trends, or make generalizations that explain the behavior of men and nations throughout recorded time. If the historian did not attempt to perform these two all-important functions, he would become nothing more than a mere chronicler—a diary keeper—and consequently the pages of human history would read just like an accountant's ledger and be just about as interesting to the layman.

The historian is constantly searching for basic factors or principles of human existence by studying ever changing and oftentimes vague historical materials. For those bygone human events that he uncovers, the historian seeks to discover underlying causes and meaning. He

---

National Geographic, Vol. 130, No. 5 (November 1966). The article pertains to the discovery by Louis Leakey of "homo habilis," a form estimated to be two million years old.

[2] See Appendix C for a chart showing the relative time spans of geological history and "human" history.

must continually search for the answer as to why something happened, trying to understand the past in order to better cope with the present. In a sense, due to the fact that he is seeking a basic understanding of human existence and behavior, the historian is something of a philosopher, for he is concerned with an ultimate. But his is a philosophy that rests on some concrete facts, not solely on ideas or thought processes alone. The noted European historian, Johan Huizinga, has very ably emphasized this concept, positing that history is an intellectual activity, but one which is very much grounded in fact and reality.[3] Hence, the historian "philosophizes" the past in order to more satisfactorily explain it. And at the same time he makes possible a more thorough philosophizing of the present, should someone desire to do so.

We have now arrived at the point where we can further clarify our original definition: History is the interpretive study of the recorded fact of bygone human beings and societies, the purpose of which study is to develop an understanding of human actions, not only in the past but for the present as well.

Such was not always the case. History in its present form is a fairly young field of study. It developed as a distinct field during the eighteenth and nineteenth centuries, a direct result of the liberating influence of the writings of philosophical giants in the seventeenth century. The newly recognized field of history reflected their philosophical beliefs. Prior to that time history was a branch of grammar in the medieval Quadrivium and Trivium—the classical seven arts curriculum of the Carolingian Palace School over a thousand years ago.

Writing at a time when man was first beginning to discover the various laws that explain the physical world, these philosophers of the Enlightenment reflected the prevailing optimism of their age. Heretofore unknown laws of the natural order were now discovered; why could there not also be various laws that govern human behavior with equal validity? Going one step further, these philosophers adopted the notion that such laws did in fact exist, and that it was the purpose of the historian to discover them.[4]

Seeking a justification for their new discipline, a few advocates of history looked forward to the day when history would develop into a pure science. Some historians believed that they would eventually

---

[3] Johan Huizinga, "A Definition of the Concept of History," *Philosophy and History: Essays Presented to Ernst Cassirer*, eds. Raymond Klibansky and H. J. Paton (New York: Harper & Row, Publishers, 1963). This particular essay is recommended to all students of history.

[4] An excellent brief essay on the significance of the Enlightenment on the development of history as a separate discipline is found in Patrick Gardiner, *Theories of History* (Glencoe, Illinois: The Free Press, 1959), Author's Introduction to the work.

discover laws explaining humanity that would have the same force and validity as those laws governing the physical world. Science was king. Hence, the historian, in an attempt to give his discipline status, mistakenly referred to it as a "social science."

This viewpoint is totally incorrect. Science deals with concrete things that can be touched, weighed, measured, and evaluated under laboratory conditions. Science deals with concrete, verifiable objects. History, on the other hand, does not deal with materials that can be touched, weighed, and measured. History is inferential, i.e., it infers the past on the basis of partially known facts. True, the historian makes use of some concrete materials in his work, such as documents, diaries, newspapers, and contemporary accounts in his investigations, but from these he must infer the past. He cannot weigh or measure these materials as the scientist can weigh or measure his materials. The historian can never know the past with complete certainty. He can never formulate laws having the same merit or authenticity of a scientific law of the physical universe.

Those who would attempt to make of history a pure science according to the then prevailing notions of the Enlightenment would in effect make science their god.[5] According to this belief, anything that is not totally scientific is of an inferior order. But the position is at best a tenuous one. The scientific method applies to the sciences—to physics, chemistry, and biology. It does not apply to man in his social context. Science may affect and influence man extrinsically, but science has nothing to offer to man in developing his humanity. The so-called social sciences and the exact sciences are different disciplinary areas. Their subject matter is entirely different, and their methodology is partially different. One is not better than the other; they operate in separate spheres. Not being of the same order, they cannot be compared, unless one believes that apples and oranges can be compared.

The historian does make some use of scientific methodology up to a point. He gathers the facts, organizes the facts, and draws conclusions from his facts. He makes hypotheses on the basis of whatever facts are definitely known. This is also what the scientist does. But the historian is unable to verify his hypotheses by experimentation; he cannot replay an historical drama in a laboratory setting—a very significant final step of the scientific method. Hence, he is not a true scientist. He is primarily a philosopher. So to our most recent definition of history we must add the salient point that history is a humanistic-type disci-

---

[5] The attempt of some early historians to liken themselves to pure scientists is very capably denounced in Jose Ortega y Gasset, *History as a System: And Other Essays Toward a Philosophy of History* (New York: W. W. Norton & Company, Inc., 1961). See particularly "History as a System."

pline, the study of human nature and human affairs, as best they can be observed.

Although it does not alter the classification of history as a distinct discipline, it should be pointed out that in certain instances the historical researcher does make some use of the tools of the exact sciences for such purposes as determining the authenticity of old documents and ascertaining the age of a document by means of paper, water mark, or ink analysis. This is strictly a laboratory technique that aids the historian in collecting his facts and determining their reliability. But science is of no direct help to the historian in the performance of his primary function, which is to interpret—to discover or formulate laws, patterns, and trends in an attempt to explain human behavior and events.

History makes no claim that it provides solutions for problems; it attempts to identify problems and to point out why they occurred when they did and how they did. History studies the human past, a rather mysterious and confusing conglomeration of apparently disordered fact that seems to be governed by sheer contingency and chance (some historians have adopted this viewpoint). It is concerned with people throughout recorded time, and as a result the historian must possess a thorough knowledge of human nature. He must always make provisions for the motivation of historical events. And how does one subject something like a hypothesized motivation to the scientific method?

Thus, the historian cannot be a strict determinist, i.e., hold that an inflexible set of environmental factors inexorably determine human behavior, and still be able to perform his function. Otherwise, there would be no value in studying man's behavior in the past because it could not ever be altered: Man would be incapable of learning from his past errors. The historian cannot permit himself the mistake of isolating a particular person or event. All historical happenings must be considered from a broad, world outlook. The historian must firmly believe in the "solidarity of the human race" concept, so ably expounded by the nineteenth-century Spanish philosopher, Donoso Cortes. For if he did not, he would be unable to give various historical events their proper significance in the story of the human race. And our historian must be in a position to make solid value judgments concerning the conduct of those historical subjects that he is considering. Otherwise, an understanding of those subjects is lacking.

History seeks to understand the human past in an effort to better understand an ever changing present, with the ambitious hope that such an understanding will provide worthwhile guidelines for future use. The greater the knowledge possessed by the historian of all facets of human behavior, the greater should be his understanding of the events which he is attempting to evaluate. Consequently, the truly competent historian must necessarily possess a working knowledge of psychology, philosophy, sociology, political science, economics, and some sort of a moral or theological system. The true historian, to borrow the terminology of the medical profession, is not a specialist; he is a general practitioner. He cannot compartmentalize the various areas of human knowledge and behavior that apply to man as man. He cannot fragment human existence. If he is going to adequately explain past human activities he must be knowledgeable in all disciplines that are concerned with human behavior. He may, however, emphasize the role of one or more of these disciplines in shaping human behavior. But the historian must be equipped to integrate the various artificial divisions of human knowledge.

The professional historian is also something of a detective—but a detective by remote control. He must know how to use clues (documents) in order to reconstruct the story of mankind, just as the detective seeks out and utilizes clues in an attempt to reconstruct a crime. But the reconstruction on the part of the historian is on a far more grandiose scale; it must take into account many more variables, and it possesses the added complexity of pertaining to actions which took place hundreds or perhaps thousands of years in the past.

As a result of these difficulties, the historian must exercise a tremendous degree of precision and care in selecting and organizing his documents.[6] A tiny slip could be compounded over centuries into an error of great magnitude. The historian must also look for the motivation for whatever he is investigating. This is his interpretation of events. However, it cannot be held with complete certitude. The past undoubtedly shapes the present. This is a demonstrable reality. But the present, through its interpretation of the past, shapes the past also, at least in terms of the present's understanding of the past. The historian is the creature of his own time and culture. Even with a superhuman effort at complete objective detachment he cannot help but subconsciously "adjust" the past somewhat to meet his own personal standards and convictions. However, this is where the broad knowledge of human nature must enter the picture and influence his thinking. The greater the knowledge possessed by the historian, the greater should be his degree of successfully attained objectivity in determining the past, and consequently the greater should be the accuracy of his interpretation of the past.

Having reconstructed and interpreted the past of mankind with

[6] An excellent advanced work is Gilbert J. Garraghan, *A Guide to Historical Method*, ed. Jean Delanglez (New York: Fordham University Press, 1946). More useful to the beginning student would be the appropriate chapters in Allan Nevins, *Gateway to History* (rev. ed.; Boston: D. C. Heath Company, 1962).

some degree of accuracy, the historian's task is not yet completed. The historian must next consider his past events in terms of their effects on later developments in order to give them proper significance. And if he so desires, the historian may then attempt to identify some trends in human events based on his understanding of the facts.

An historian is always looking for trends in human activities. But even if the historian identifies a trend with complete certitude, this does not preclude the possibility that the trend will halt at any particular future moment. In fact, by the very fact that the historian does identify a trend, he may make possible the climate of opinion that will divert or destroy that trend.

The historian is always seeking for the causes of various effects. For instance, he knows that wars occur, but a mere knowledge that wars are quite commonplace in human affairs is hardly sufficient. Everyone knows that wars exist. But the historian hopes to discover why they exist. He wants to be able to state that when certain conditions are present a war is a distinct possibility. Again, he will never be able to reduce his causes to mathematical formulae. But his effort to discover the "why" of things is a real merit and worth of history.

The field of history makes no claim that it provides the answers for a better human existence, but it at least makes an attempt to find the answers if they do exist. History wisely does not guarantee that mistakes will not be repeated in the future, but it does point out those mistakes that have been made and repeated in the past.

In the final analysis, man is a free agent; he possesses some control over his environment and activities. The world is not a test tube and mankind is not a controlled laboratory experiment. The future is unpredictable but not unmanageable, for the more knowledge mankind can possess concerning himself, the greater will be his chances for developing a better future. This is the intrinsic worth of history as a discipline.

History is the humanistic, interpretive study of past human society, the purpose of which is to gain insight into the present with the fervent hope of perhaps influencing a more favorable future course for the human race.

PROBLEMS IN THE STUDY
OF HISTORY

2

It has already been pointed out that history at the introductory survey course level is too frequently taught or regarded as a memorization course in names, dates, and events. This attitude quite obviously reflects neither the purpose nor the function of the discipline of history. The names, dates, and events of history are nothing more than the tools employed by the historian to serve his end, just as the hammer and saw are the tools of the carpenter or mathematical knowledge is a tool of the research scientist.

The historian must use historical fact in order to gain some understanding of the present if he hopes to obtain some insight into the future. The same is true of the student in a history course. The facts of history provide the necessary foundation stones for a real inquiry into the nature of man. With this in mind, the problems that the beginning college student of history will encounter are presented below.

1. CAUSE-AND-EFFECT RELATIONSHIPS

One of the most difficult problems encountered in the study of history concerns how to accurately assess the causes for various historical occurrences. A proper study of history should result in an awareness of how attitudes, ideas, and events flow and develop throughout recorded time. The historian attempts to discover the causes or reasons for these attitudes, ideas, and events. He inquires into their interrelationship.

It is hardly sufficient to state that, because the battleship *Maine* was blown up in Cuba shortly before the Spanish-American War erupted, the *Maine* disaster was responsible for the ensuing conflict. It did constitute an immediate, prior event, but this alone did not necessarily make it a cause for the war. It would be much more sensible to call the sinking of the *Maine* a cause for the war than it would be to blame the conflict on the assassination of President McKinley because of its chronological placement.

The historian must search out real and substantiated causes; he cannot content himself with using immediate, prior, and convenient incidents to explain subsequent events.[1] No doubt the coming of the Spanish-American War was the effect of something. And the historian must determine what this something is. He fully recognizes that there is no single isolated cause or simple explanation for any of the complex events of history. Life is not that simple.

As matters turn out, the sinking of the battleship *Maine* was a factor in bringing about the war but not just because it immediately preceded the conflict. To discover this, the historian must delve deeper into the background of the war. It is soon discovered that whether or not the Spanish authorities in Cuba actually sank the vessel is irrelevant (it is still unknown) as a causal factor. The American public jumped to the conclusion that Spain was guilty of sinking the vessel, and a strong anti-Spanish opinion developed in the nation. The historian, then, has to analyze the reasons why Americans were so willing to accept the sinking of the *Maine* as justification for seeking war with Spain. And with this intent the historian discovers such factors as the "yellow press," McKinley's bowing to vested interests, and the resurrection of the Black Legend—all of which aid in explaining the war temper of the American people.

Behind the obvious, there are causes for the Spanish-American War—and for all other historical events as well—that must be sought out just as the detective builds up clues piecemeal in reconstructing a crime. Some causes may be remote; they may superficially appear unrelated. But causes can never be ignored simply because they are not obvious. Nor should the extension of causal factors into the past imply that we should blame every human mishap on the biblical fact that Adam ate the forbidden fruit and that we may shrug it off. What is meant is that it is extremely difficult to understand anything in an historical sense until one has first acquired a storehouse of historical

---

[1] The beginning student may desire to probe more deeply into the various aspects of "cause" and "effect." Any good logic text would provide such material. By way of example, see Irving M. Copi, *Introduction to Logic* (2nd ed.; New York: The Macmillan Company, 1961), especially Chapter XII.

fact plus a knowledge of the various disciplines dealing with human behavior.

Causes are exceedingly difficult to assess. The historian must be very careful to avoid an over-reliance on convenient, but not necessarily adequate, explanations. Every human event is complex; a multitude of forces, some known and others unknown, shape and influence it. But this does not mean that every explanation of a human event should be cluttered with reams of trivial data.

To get to the heart of the matter, cause and effect relationships pertain to nothing more than plain, basic, logical method. Both the professional historian and the survey course history student must be able to think logically and systematically if they hope to derive the full benefit from the discipline of history.

2. TIME PERSPECTIVE

The student must also be cognizant of the significance of time and the problems associated with it, both in span and chronology.[2] It is not humanly possible to conceptualize adequately the vast immensity of time, but an honest effort is a necessary prerequisite for the development of historical mindedness. An appreciation of time sequence is imperative for a thorough understanding of cause and effect relationships. Hence, dates become important tools of the trade.

The placing of events in proper sequential order is normally far more important than the exact dates of the events themselves. The degree of exactitude of the date of any event depends upon the circumstances surrounding it. For instance, the month and the day of the year 800 A.D. when Charlemagne was crowned emperor by the Pope is relatively unimportant. The fact that the event took place on Christmas Day is perhaps interesting and reflective of the medieval religious spirit but not really essential. The month of the year 1588 when the Spanish Armada set sail for England is very important, whereas the exact day of the month is not. For in this illustration, the knowledge of the season during which the Armada sailed has an absolute bearing on an understanding of the tremendous losses which the Spaniards incurred due to seasonal storms in the North Sea. During the kaleidescopic events of the French nation in 1789, exact days of the month are extremely important. And in an event like the Japanese attack on Pearl Harbor and the fixing of responsibility for

[2] Chronological tables are often useful tools for survey course students. They enable one to grasp pictorially the idea of time perspective. Incidentally, the formulation of such tables by the student is often a good study technique. See Appendix C for chronological tables of the Western world.

the lack of American defenses, it may be necessary to study the day hour by hour. Again, this minuteness of study would depend on the nature of the historical inquiry.

Then, too, the circumstances surrounding the event under consideration will usually determine the minuteness to be observed in placing it within a given time period. The pre-Cambrian period would be dated in terms of millions of years. To state that Columbus discovered America within the past million years would be entirely devoid of meaning. Mature judgment should prevail when considering the degree of exactitude for dates, but chronology must be strictly observed under all circumstances.

3. OBJECTIVITY AND TOLERANCE

By far one of the most important functions and the greatest difficulties in the study of history concerns objectivity and tolerance. Objectivity in the study and interpretation of historical data involves the use of historical facts without personal bias or prejudice. Tolerance means giving a full and impartial hearing to an opposing view and respecting that view, provided it is derived honestly. The attainment of objectivity and tolerance, of course, is limited to the restrictions of human nature.

Perhaps when the historian is arguing in favor of objectivity and tolerance he is really arguing on the plane of the proverbial two-headed coin that reads on both sides: "This side is up." For objectivity and tolerance are both necessary for the proper writing and studying of history as they are the end results from its study. Objectivity and tolerance are at one and the same time both cause and effect. Also, it should be pointed out that one will never be able to write and interpret history properly unless he first learns how to study it properly.

By the very fact that history can never be correctly classified as a laboratory science (as has already been indicated in the previous chapter), the historian must admit that there might be various logical, valid interpretations of the same historical event. His problem is to find the interpretation which best accords with the generally accepted, factual information available—there may be more than one. The objective historian must respect the opinions of his peers, provided, of course, that these opinions are methodically formulated, even though he might wholeheartedly and vigorously disagree with these opinions from a strictly personal viewpoint. Such an attitude implies an at least tacit acceptance of tolerance. And professional historians, fortunately, are usually the guardians of each other's intellectual honesty, occasionally to the point of some rather fine hairsplitting.

Couple this accepted tolerance with an honest attempt toward objectivity (realizing, of course, that no human being is capable of complete objectivity—a decided but unavoidable drawback to the discipline) and history, of all fields of human knowledge, is in a position to make one of the greatest contributions to the general education of an individual. It is not the acquisition of historical fact, but rather the acceptance of the historical technique that can bring this development to its logical fruition. Unfortunately, in the survey history course it is more often the historical fact than the historical technique which is taught. Nonetheless, an individual thoroughly grounded in the proper study of history is capable of doing much to lessen the amount of bigotry and prejudice in the world.

The student should be cautioned, however, against accepting too readily any historical interpretation, regardless of its claims toward objectivity. No matter how intellectually honest the historian might be, whatever he writes is the product of his own environment, education, and value structure. His interpretations are the results of his personal beliefs and outlook on life. It is impossible for these influences not to affect his writings grossly.[3] Some of the most sincere individuals who have taken up the writing of history have been the most incorrect. Unfortunately the historical technique can very readily be employed as a two-edged sword. One very proper blade of this hypothetical sword cuts away at bigotry and prejudice, but the other blade is quite capable of increasing it.

There are certain problems attendant even to the proper utilization of history. Every generation and every culture has its own opinion as to what worth and importance should be attached to the past (this is very interestingly brought out in George Orwell's *1984*). This depends entirely on prevailing values and moral structure. History is always interpreted by the present. Obviously, then, the nature of the present will determine one's understanding of the past. A pagan present would afford one picture of human history, whereas a present highly imbued with Judeo-Christian beliefs would portray a completely different picture. Both cultures would be utilizing the same canvas and the same paint, but the brush strokes would be quite different. Yet within their respective contexts, both of these societies could create their own objective versions of the past. And necessarily, the end results of their studies would not represent the same human fabric.

[3] The following works contain useful accounts of this difficulty: J. Huizinga, "A Definition of the Concept of History," *Philosophy and History: Essays Presented to Ernst Cassirer*, eds. Raymond Klibansky and H. J. Paton (New York: Harper & Row, Publishers, 1963), Patrick Gardiner, *Theories of History* (Glencoe, Illinois: The Free Press, 1959), especially pp. 344–355, and Herbert Muller, *The Uses of the Past: Profiles of Former Societies* (New York: Oxford University Press, 1957).

If honestly attempted objective history suffers from such a serious drawback, one can readily imagine the degree of difficulty associated with the use of history for nonobjective purposes—the other blade of our hypothetical two-edged sword. For if slanted, history-writing can easily be utilized to cultivate bigotry and prejudice because of the simple fact that historical writings are capable of propagandization. A case in point would be the modern communistic historians. And it cannot be stressed too greatly that deliberately propagandized history is really not history at all.

Nevertheless, a very serious difficulty presents itself, and it is compounded by the fact that there is a fine dividing line between an erroneous interpretation or an unintentional error in methodology on the one hand, and a deliberate attempt to propagandize under the guise of historical objectivity on the other hand. The effects on the reader would be equally damaging in either case. Both professional historian and student of history must be constantly on guard against the danger of unreliable materials, interpretations, and conclusions.

4. PHILOSOPHY OF HISTORY

The historian, if he is going to be something other than a mere compiler of unrelated fact, must concern himself with formulating a direction or general course of human events and developments. He must conduct a conscientious and legitimate search for meaning in history. And the history student, if he is going to become something other than a mere memorizer of meaningless, confused fact, must be fully aware of this concern and this search and appreciate its value.

The practicing historian, of course, must always be careful not to formulate his patterns to the point of overgeneralization (even though some generalization is necessary in the study of history).[4] When the historian posits his generalizations both he and the history student must accept them for just what they are: They do not apply to every set of circumstances; they may not even provide a complete explanation for the items under consideration. The historian is incapable of tying human affairs into neat little packages (even though he must occasionally fight the tendency to do so), for he is dealing with a constantly changing story, an unpredictable human will, and enormous gaps in his own knowledge.

Nor should the historian deceive himself by claiming the ability to predict the future (occasionally one succumbs to the temptation). This historian is not a soothsayer; he does not possess a crystal ball. But he is able to make some reasonably reliable estimates concerning

[4] See Louis Gottschalk (ed.), *Generalization in the Writing of History* (Chicago: The University of Chicago Press, 1963), for an introduction to the immense complexity of this problem.

the course of present events, in light of past developments, and in this manner he can shed some possible light on the future. Thus, philosophy of history is an attempt to organize and account for the human past in such a manner that it becomes meaningful and worthwhile.

The philosophy of history, in its origin, development, and scope, will be developed more fully in the next chapter. But at this point it should be indicated that there are a number of concepts which must be adhered to by both the historian and the student of history if they are to develop a meaningful philosophy of history. For example, it seems that the solidarity of the human race concept is a *sine qua non.* All men in all ages, regardless of location or stage of civilization, have some effect on one another. They are all members of the human family, and there is a certain unity in the human experience. Another example is the acceptance of a value system, a subject that is to be considered in the following unit.

5. A VALUE SYSTEM

Every human being has his own personal outlook on life, which is based on his education, his environment, and his experiences. His understanding of what has preceded him is conditioned by this outlook. Consequently the discipline of history must be considered in the light of some sort of a value system, and that value system is determined by the culture in which the historian lives. To render any sort of a judgment means to compare an action against an already accepted mode of behavior. This does not mean that an interpretation of history must reflect only one particular theological system, but rather a moral, humanistic, esthetic set of principles based upon the cumulative contributions of Western civilization operating within the framework of the Judeo-Christian tradition. For such is the heritage of Western man and the generally accepted value structure of the Western world.

It would be rather ridiculous to consider American history in the light of Hindu standards, unless, of course, one who adhered to Hindu standards were doing the writing for Hindu readers. It would be equally ridiculous to interpret the history of Pomerania in terms of the value structure of the American Great Awakening. We have our own cultural heritage that must be employed to interpret properly and to understand ourselves. We must interpret, as far as is humanly possible, the conduct of others first by their own standards, and having done so we can compare them with ourselves. This approach in no way restricts the activities of the historian; it is the only manner in which he can properly perform his function. And it might be pointed out that regardless of the cultural framework within which the historian is operating, ample latitude is provided for varying shades of opinions and attitudes within his adopted center of reference.

A little earlier it was suggested that there are certain widely held values that are peculiar to the Judeo-Christian tradition of Western civilization—the framework in which an overwhelming majority of Americans are operating. These values are relatively simple to ascertain. They include the concept of human dignity and the priceless quality of human existence. They include a recognition of both good and evil in the world and the fundamental opposition between these two forces. And they include the fact that with every claimed right or privilege there are corresponding obligations. No human being lives his life in a vacuum. History affords a multitude of illustrations of human dignity and deprivation, of moral growth and moral disintegration, and of countless other comparisons.

All of these concepts and many more reflect the absolute necessity of a solidly grounded value structure for the success of any human endeavor. History without a value system cannot be interpreted or explained. An accepted frame of reference is necessary before the rendering of judgments can even take place. How can we possibly claim that a given action is good or bad unless we first have some idea of what the words "good" and "bad" signify? Our only alternative would be to claim amorality, and again we would only succeed in plunging the discipline backwards into a meaningless void.

There is one very serious difficulty arising out of the value system concept. As has already been indicated historians are prone to interpret past events in terms of their own social and cultural structure. This is most proper and commendable for purposes of comparison, but it cannot, under any circumstances, be utilized as an evaluative norm. Otherwise we would lose the flavor of the past. Nor can the knowledge of the present be used in assessing causes for past events. It is rather easy to be a Sunday morning quarterback, since all facts are then known. Causes as we see them are not necessarily causes as the past saw them. Bygone man must be interpreted in terms of his own, not the interpreting historian's, value structure. Afterward, conclusions may be drawn by comparison with the modern value structure. Only by evaluating the achievements and failures of mankind according to the acceptable standards of the time when they actually took place can the historian hope to acquire some understanding of these standards for the present day. Again, a plea is being made for tolerance, for this is a legitimate function of history.

6. A UNIQUE DISCIPLINE

History possesses a unique role as a discipline primarily because it is a very encompassing discipline. It is not strictly a social science, or a behavioral science, or one of the humanities, and definitely not an exact science. Yet it is partially all of these areas of knowledge contained in one complex, integrated package. Consequently history provides an excellent mechanism for the general or broad-scope education of an individual in that it aptly demonstrates the correlation and integration of all branches of human knowledge. It could not be otherwise, for history is concerned with the study of man in all of his endeavors. An individual can only hope to truly educate himself in the direction of the "Know Thyself" maxim by considering man in his totality.

This demonstration of the unique role of history as an encompassing discipline is exceedingly important in an age when bodies of human knowledge are continually being fragmented and compartmentalized owing to the tremendous growth of knowledge over the past few centuries. History is quite capable of providing a trunk line for all human knowledge. Within its framework, any and every discipline can and should be considered.

Some remarkable progress has been made along these lines in recent years, e.g., American Studies programs, History of Ideas programs, and History of Science programs, plus a host of integrated approaches. This capacity comprises an ambitious task for history, but history is a rather ambitious discipline. It provides the basis for understanding the structure and development of the total human being.

Of course the uniqueness of history as a discipline creates some rather serious problems for the student in an introductory survey course, in that he generally does not yet possess a wide range of knowledge to integrate. But he has some, and over a few short years it will grow tremendously. A lower division history student should begin his task of acquiring a complete, integrated education as quickly as possible. Otherwise, the longer it is put off, the more difficult it will become.

One might well become a veritable storehouse of encyclopedic knowledge, but this in itself does not constitute an educated individual. One of the principal characteristics of a truly educated person is his ability to integrate and correlate knowledge. The educated person possesses a broad and tolerant view on life. As he cannot obtain this perspective from specializing in a single, isolated discipline, he requires a total picture of humanity. The unique discipline of history aids the student in realizing this extremely worthwhile objective.

PHILOSOPHIES OF HISTORY

3

The term "philosophy of history" pertains to that particular branch of historical study which places major emphasis on the ultimate course of human civilization. A philosophy of history is the personal interpretation and judgment of the individual who is formulating it. It cannot be verified any more than can the pure philosophical systems of such great thinkers as Descartes, Locke, and Kant. Its only validity is in the mind of its creator and the individuals who choose to accept it. A philosophy of history is a systematizing of human knowledge and thought within the realm of historical fact. This systematizing is acceptable only to its originator and his disciples. Nonetheless, a philosophy of history, if logically formulated, proposes considerable food for thought. It provides one explanation of human events, and it also provides the real justification of history as a discipline. For a philosophy of history systematizes the vast bulk of fact comprising the human past, and in giving this fact order it also gives it meaning. Occasionally, a philosophy of history exerts a tremendous influence on the shaping of the world, e.g., the dialectical materialism notion in the writings of Karl Marx—yes, Marx was a philosopher of history whose system has found political implementation in the modern world.

Every student of history should possess a fundamental knowledge of the various major interpretations of history. In outline form this is the purpose of the present chapter. It is hoped that the beginning student of history will thus be in a better position to consider history in its true perspective. It is further hoped that the student will become equipped to intelligently choose, develop, or adapt his own philosophy of history more discriminately.

1. THE CYCLICAL VIEW

The first widespread interpretation of history was the cyclical theory. In Western culture the cyclical theory existed in dominant form from the time of Herodotus (484–425 B.C.) to the time of Christ.[1] According to the cyclical viewpoint all human events occur in cycles. Names, dates, and persons may change, but periodically what happened before will happen again and for the same reasons. This applies equally to nation-states and to epochs. We have all heard the trite statement that history repeats itself. Those who make such a statement, whether they realize it or not, are reflecting the cyclical theory, for according to this theory, history does in fact repeat itself.

However, cyclicalism standing alone is not a philosophy of history in the true meaning of the term. A philosophy of history presupposes a beginning, middle course, and end or realization for the human experience. A repeating cycle is meaningless: It has no realization, and it denies that man is capable of improvement. It is merely proceeding to its own beginning. But the cyclical idea, when combined with various other notions, could and did result in some rather interesting and influential philosophies of history.

The cyclical theory was predominant in the ancient world when mankind possessed no real knowledge of the universe or the role that he was destined to play in it. In a primitive culture everything but the immediate present was relatively insignificant. The primitive mind possessed no thorough understanding of time perspective. By way of illustration consider for a moment the effect you would have on a toddler if you told him that something is to be done next month or next year. He only understands the present.

So the cyclical theory made no real contribution to man's knowledge concerning his role in this life. The importance of the cyclical theory lies in the fact that it was the first theory, later synthesized with other concepts. But along came Christianity, and the Christians of Europe experienced a considerable amount of difficulty in interpreting the Messianic promise in terms of the cyclical theory. Christians regarded the coming of Christ as a unique event. It was not something

[1] This does not imply that there are no longer any cyclical historians. Oswald Spengler and Arnold Toynbee are both members of the school. Also, I am excluding any consideration of cyclical theories in Eastern thought, and in that area, cyclicalism has traditionally enjoyed more widespread acceptance than in the West. An excellent work, tracing cyclicalism historically in both East and West, is Grace Cairns, *Philosophies of History: Meeting of East and West in Cycle-Pattern Theories of History* (New York: Philosophical Library, Inc., 1962).

that would be repeated every two, three, or four hundred years, for if it would repeat itself periodically it would become commonplace and thereby lose much of its significance. Thus, the cyclical theory witnessed a rather abrupt end in Western thought as the dominant historical pattern. In altered form it remains to the present day, but it has been tempered considerably by combination with other ingredients.

2. THE PROVIDENTIAL VIEW

After the influence of the cyclical theory lessened, the next dominant interpretation was the providential viewpoint of history. The view had existed among certain peoples during the Old Testament era, notably the Hebrews, but it had been overshadowed by cyclicalism. The providential view was quite widespread during the church-oriented Middle Ages. Throughout this period every human and every natural occurrence was explained in terms of an intervening divine providence. Catastrophes, whether they were wars or earthquakes, were readily interpreted as divinely ordained punishment for some alleged human wrongdoing. Peace and well-being were generally understood as positive signs that a divine providence was quite well satisfied with the activities of his creatures.

Man, it appeared, had practically no control over his own environment, but this did not greatly disturb the "other world" mentality of the Middle Ages. For the providential viewpoint provided great security for a nonscientific people who possessed real knowledge neither of causation nor of the physical universe in which they were living. The medieval man did not believe it possible to exercise any control over his world.

One of the leading exponents and pioneers of the providential theory of history was Augustine. A transitional figure, Augustine attempted to synthesize pagan cyclical thought and Greco-Roman intellectual achievements with the basic ideas of Christianity. The result of this attempt is a combination of cyclicalism and providence in history. Augustine's *De Civitas Dei* (*The City of God*) is a philosophy of history. According to this work the world is made up of two symbolic cities: a city of good and a city of evil, representing God on the one side and the devil on the other. Human history consists of a recording of the death struggle between these two opposing powers for ascendancy. The end of this struggle will be the final determination of either eternal salvation or eternal damnation for the entire human race.

Man is relegated to the role of a pawn in this game of high stakes. Quite naturally, he is deeply concerned about the outcome of the struggle, but he is extremely limited in doing anything about it. Obviously wanting the forces of good to win because of the promise of eternal happiness, he leads a good life in order to identify with his choice of combatants. But his world is strictly a battleground for eternity, and forces other than mankind are shaping human destinies.

However, in this theory, human history has now achieved an end. The end is eternal salvation. For even though this end often appears quite uncertain—there would be battles won and battles lost by both the forces of good and evil—according to Augustine, God will win the struggle, and He will proceed to reward those human beings who have not lost faith in His abilities.

Within such a frame of reference little or no heed was paid to material achievements. No material thing on the face of this earth was recognized as having any real importance. The earth was strictly a waiting room for eternity. Thus, the providential viewpoint was ideally suited for a spiritual-oriented Christian medieval Europe. It satisfied the existing cultural milieu—as philosophies of history are so prone to do. In terms of material or physical advancement for humanity the view is stagnant. This does not mean to imply that the Middle Ages witnessed no material advances. The unfortunate "Dark Ages" terminology does not do justice to the period. However, material achievements usually took a back seat in the existing value structure. And those material achievements being made almost always reflected the prevailing spiritualism.

3. THE PROGRESS VIEW

But with the birth of scientific interest and inquiry, and with the breaking down of institutionalized Christian unity due to the developments of the Renaissance and Reformation eras, the rise of a materialistically minded middle class, and the discoveries of such great scientific minds as those of Newton, Leibnitz, and Galileo, Europe took on a new set of values. And out of this new set of values a new theory of history was being formulated.

The cyclical theory had been superseded by the Christian providence view. Now the providence view was under attack because of the great advances taking place in the furtherance of human knowledge. Despite the prevailing teachings of the Church, Europe was becoming progressively more materialistic in outlook. It was becoming conscious of man as man. It was beginning to think that man might possibly have some control over his destiny and environment. It was discovering some of the secrets of the universe. Natural laws, not divine intervening providence, appeared to govern good and ill fortune. Europe was beginning to think in terms of notable advances in human existence on earth as well as of eternal salvation.

The prevailing providence view was tempered somewhat by such thinkers as Bossuet and Vico, but it was left to the universal genius of Gottfried Leibnitz to introduce a new dominant historical theory. All of these developments took place around the beginning of the eighteenth century. This new theory, which was adopted almost universally by historians, was named the progress theory. According to its principal thesis, the human race is continually getting better and better. It is progressing, becoming more civilized with the passage of each new generation (or as Voltaire would put it, mankind is becoming more and more like Voltaire).[2]

The new theory of progress, imbued with the widespread optimism of the Age of the Enlightenment, placed complete faith in human abilities rather than in divine abilities. It holds that each new generation builds upon the achievements of each preceding generation, and that as a result it must be better (Leibnitz's law of continuity) because it has more with which to start. And this is a gradual, continual process; there are no halts, and there are no sudden surges of high achievement. This assumption, according to the more rigid adherents of the theory, quickly develops into an inevitable law of nature. Mankind is required by nature to progress; no choice is had in the matter.

If, as the progress adherents hold, mankind is continually and inevitably progressing, the question immediately arises as to the ultimate end of this progress—if indeed, such an end actually exists. Is it indefinite progress, or is there some definite goal to be realized, either on earth or in eternity? By no means agreed on the answer to this question, the adherents of the progress viewpoint fragmented into various schools.

Some adherents posit indefinite progress strictly within the material realm; to these individuals progress is endless. Others predict the eventual realization of a utopian society on earth, at which point progress must necessarily cease, for perfection will have been achieved by mankind. Still others believe that mankind will continually progress on earth but that there is an end to human history and that the real goal of the human race is to be found in eternity. Members of this latter group will blend in a greater or lesser quantity of providence

---

[2] An excellent work that traces the transition from providence to progress is John Bury, *The Idea of Progress* (London: Macmillan and Company, Ltd., 1921). There is no single work pertaining to the United States which covers the entire subject. However, an excellent work for the time period considered is Arthur A. Ekirch, *The Idea of Progress in America, 1815–1860* (New York: Peter Smith, 1951).

with their progress views, depending on their personal theological convictions. Regardless of the type of progress put forth, the idea of progress has become very much a part of our way of life in the twentieth century.

The progress view of history is practically universal in the modern world. Of course, there are some prophets of doom, especially in an age of nuclear weaponry, and these prophets are able to make quite a case for their respective positions. But modern man is basically optimistic. He lives the greater portion of his present planning for and dreaming about a better future. Modern man has adapted to his peculiar environment; he has mastered the technique of pushing aside the uncertainties of life (at least on the surface of things) and tends to look upon himself as an immortal, indestructible, unique character—sort of a twentieth-century Nietzschean superman. Needless to state, such an attitude carries with it a considerable degree of frustration, as most critics of the present age are quick to indicate. But nonetheless, this attitude of modern man is widespread. It is the logical conclusion to the theory of indefinite progress, and perhaps only it can give man the crutch he needs, having lost the security he had under the providence view.

An exceedingly influential progress view of history in the twentieth century is the one formulated by Karl Marx during the 1800's. Popularly regarded only as the founder of modern communism, Marx is rarely thought of as a philosopher of history except in academic circles. Yet the *Communist Manifesto* is a philosophy of history. The basis of the Marxian system is found in the mundane writings of the German idealistic philosopher, Hegel, and is known as the dialectic. The Hegelian dialectic was utilized by Marx, who claimed to have discovered an immutable and universal law of human history, which would eventually reach fruition within time. Today the system of Karl Marx is commonly referred to as the Communist dialectic.

The history of mankind, according to Marx, is the story of class struggle. Class relations are based on the mode of production of the individual—the role a person plays in the economic structure—and the productive role is the determining factor in history. Man is primarily a producing animal, and his economic status in relation to other men not only determines his social class, but also it is the determining factor of human nature. The existing dominant class always breeds its opposition because it is forcing the subservient class to put more of itself into what it is producing than what it receives for its effort. Therefore, there exists alienation, and the result is conflict, out of which a new class structure will develop. Marx even has an equation for this class struggle: Thesis plus antithesis equals synthesis. For example, the medieval aristocracy created its own opposition in the form of downtrodden serfs, but out of this structure the rising middle class emerged as a completely new class. Everything is in a constant state of flux, and this is both good and inevitable. For according to the dialectic of Marxian communism, everything is as it should be at all times. (This attitude renders it impossible to argue effectively with a confirmed Marxist.)

As the various phases of this class struggle of mankind are realized, and a new class structure is being created, progress is being achieved. The end of this bloody and drawn-out class struggle will be, according to Marx, the end of all struggle due to the abolition of all classes and the end of self-alienation; mankind will achieve complete freedom in a perfect communistic society. With this development, the Marxian equation eventually runs out of steam and ceases to exist.

The adherent of the Marxian theory of progress is quite a secure person. An inevitable law has determined the eventual realization of his system, given the condition, of course, that the Marxian "law" is valid. The Marxian theory, which holds sway over a large portion of the modern-day world, is simply a typical progress view of history with a utopian climax on earth, but it is one that has been adjusted, adapted, and put into practice by a powerful political organization.

Another area where the progress theory is highly influential is within the United States. Admittedly, democracy rests on no concise, formalized philosophical system, and progress in America is based on no formalized philosophy of history. But progress is an integral part of modern American society—one need only to listen to the politicians talk about it during election years. What are the "Square Deals," "New Deals," "New Nationalisms," "New Freedoms," "New Frontiers," and "Great Societies" but various twentieth-century attempts by political leaders to implement a program of progress for the American people? What successful politician does not talk about moving ahead, improving life, etc., and what audience does not applaud such speeches?

4. MISCELLANEOUS PHILOSOPHIES OF HISTORY

The cyclical view, the providential view, and the progress view comprise the three major historical interpretations concerning the course of mankind that have been developed to date. History has also been subjected to various other interpretations, none of which, however, was or is as influential as those already described above. For the most part, other interpretations are adaptations and combinations of the three major theories. Still, they deserve at least brief mention, and the student of history would do well to be aware of them. What follows is a representative sampling of these viewpoints.[3]

Oswald Spengler likened human cultures to the life cycles of human beings. All cultures are destined to follow identical patterns of progress and decay. History, according to Spengler, must be considered through the eyes of the biologist. The view is cyclical, for historical time is simply the registration of the life process. Although the view is pessimistic, repudiating the progress view at a time when that view was flourishing, Spengler's work was widely read until Arnold Toynbee superseded it in 1927.

Toynbee accepted part of Spengler's notions but was actually writing to repudiate them. He adopted Spengler's "cultures," which he termed "civilizations." These civilizations are people considered collectively, and they are subject to natural and biological laws. They all follow the same cycles. But unlike Spengler, Toynbee held that this does not necessarily continue. Civilization can progress, building upon past achievements as it goes along. The key is challenge and response. If a civilization is presented with a challenge to which it is able to respond adequately, growth occurs. And as a corollary to this, creative minorities therefore stimulate the growth of the civilization of which they are a part. Much more optimistic than Spengler, Toynbee provides for progress in his view of history, blending the cyclical and progress views together.

Another thinker, August Comte, viewed history as a struggle in which change must inevitably take place. Human history consists of nothing more than one long struggle to discover the heretofore unknown perfect laws of social living. These immutable laws exist, he claimed, but the human race will not necessarily discover them. Thus, the reputed father of modern sociology presented us with a potential earthly utopia as a possible end result. Comte was stating that there can be, but not necessarily will be, indefinite progress. Man possesses the capacity for progress if he can but discover it.

People such as Condorcet and Turgot held that history is the recounting of a human progression from east to west. As new civilizations develop more to the west, they are improved versions of older civilizations to the east. Progress is thereby achieved because mankind is improving; he is drawing upon the successes and failures of earlier societies in order to create a better one. This is a progress view, but it is a form of progress that is strongly determined by geography. It, too, is inevitable. The viewpoint is a curious mixture of what might be

---

[3] As yet there is no basic survey work on philosophies of history suitable for a majority of lower division history students. Examples of advanced works are found in the bibliography.

termed a limited geographical cyclicalism with progress as an end result. The cycle, incidentally, would supposedly end in the United States (both men were ardent admirers of American democracy); it would not keep circling the globe.

A minor takeoff on this geographical viewpoint is the climatic theory, of which the American, Ralph Waldo Emerson, was one notable exponent. This theory holds that superior civilizations can only develop in temperate zones. Those civilizations existing elsewhere are extremely limited in the amount of progress which they can achieve; those located in temperate zones may progress indefinitely. The reason for this is that temperature differences are held to provide a stimulus to greater activity, whereas people residing in consistently hot or cold environments become as stagnant as their surroundings.

Herbert Spencer held that history is the movement from the homogeneous to the heterogeneous—from simple tribal systems to complex urban structures and from one-celled organisms to a highly complex man. Cultures could decay and fall, just as individuals grow old and die, but the ultimate course of the human race is upward and onward. This is a form of inevitable progress, and its end is human perfection. Of course, Spencer was simply reflecting the extremely influential evolution theory as posited by Charles Darwin. His viewpoint remains quite popular to the present day and appears to be borne out by what is commonly regarded as twentieth century progress.

Hegel, a philosophical idealist, believed history to be a bloody world struggle but also, at the same time, to be a rational process. History is in a fluid state; by the process of negation it moves in the direction of the absolute concrete universal—the *Geist*. The realization of the *Geist*, or absolute world spirit, will result from the submission of all individual spirits into the collective spirit, and the divine idea—the state—will be realized on earth. The realization of the *Geist* will bring an end to the negation process. At the same time, mankind will completely realize his freedom by submerging his individuality into the state, for the universal divine idea—the *Geist*—is only realized when it becomes universally accepted by mankind. Again, this is a variance of the basic progress viewpoint.

We could go on and on, and we have only lightly touched upon the theories sampled. There are all sorts of other theories and interpretations (some are alluded to in the chapter on European historiography). A number of these theories possess some degree of merit, whereas some are totally meaningless except to their formulators. But the student must bear in mind the fact that regardless of their merit or lack of merit, they are only theories. They cannot be satisfactorily proven—even the meaningful ones. Most of them cannot be disproven either.

Be that as it may, there is real merit in attempting to discover some sense and meaning in human history. Although some of these theories appear to be ridiculous, as they most probably are, we should remain cognizant of the fact that they do represent sincere attempts (even on the part of such a confused soul as Vico) to form some order out of the apparent chaos that is the history of mankind.

Mankind can learn to profit from his previous errors. So, too, can nations profit from their past mistakes. Perfectibility is to be sought, not as an end to be achieved necessarily, but as an ideal. This is the message of the great minds in human history.

HISTORICAL WRITING: TYPES
AND TECHNIQUES

4

There are two broad categories of historical writing with which the beginning student should be thoroughly familiar. One category consists of those materials upon which the student must rely in order to acquire his historical fact. From the viewpoint of the student we may arbitrarily refer to these writings as "historical information materials." The other category is concerned with those types of writings that the student will probably be required to submit as class assignments.

1. HISTORICAL INFORMATION MATERIALS

The student of history should be familiar with, and possess a thorough working knowledge of, three basic types of historical writing that will provide him with his facts. These categories, each of which contains various forms, are: (A) primary works, both in published and in manuscript form, (B) secondary works, both published and unpublished; and (C) journal articles, which include magazine articles, newspaper accounts, and articles in the various professional historical journals.

A. *Primary Works* Primary works are original source materials for historical fact—tangible materials, which existed at the time the historical event was taking place and which aid in describing it. They include such items as eyewitness accounts, dairies, letters, and public documents (laws, treaties, hearings, court decisions, etc.). They include photographs and newsreels, as well as some of the artifacts discovered by the archaeologist. Stamps, coins, coats of arms, seals, wills, genealogical tables, in fact, just about everything that can give us some clue to the past, if it is in its original, untampered form, may be classified as primary source material.

Written original sources do not have to be in their original manuscript form. But a primary work cannot be edited, other than in organization, and still be classified as a primary work. Published collections of Bismarck's personal correspondence, for instance, are primary materials, even though the compiler has probably arranged them in some sort of order, either by chronology or by subject. But an interpretation of Bismarck's correspondence, even though material is quoted extensively from it, is not a primary source; it has been altered. Similarly, a volume of American treaties is primary material but an interpretation of American foreign policy is not. Great care should be exercised in the use of newspaper accounts. They may be primary material, but they may also editorialize, thereby giving a slant to the past that might not be entirely accurate.

The historian utilizes primary materials to acquire his facts, which he then organizes, interprets, and formulates into the reconstruction of a bygone event. He must always provide the interpretation when he is working with primary source materials.

It is highly doubtful that the beginning student of history will make much use of primary materials except, perhaps, for some of the excellent published collections now available, which might be incorporated into a term paper but which are not necessary for a good term paper. He might also make use of family records or letters, and these are classified as primary materials. But the use of primary materials even in published form is fairly well entrenched in the domain of the graduate student of history and the professional historian, and unpublished primary materials are even more their fare.

B. *Secondary Works*   The bulk of materials used by beginning history students will center around secondary source materials. As the term implies, secondary materials are one step removed from primary materials. Secondary works are the end product of the historian's use and study of primary materials, to which he has added his own organization and interpretation. This does not mean, however, that the historian acquires all of his facts for a secondary work from primary sources alone. He may rely quite heavily on primary materials, but he also consults many other secondary works and journal articles. He legitimately takes full advantage of the research of his fellow historians—and the historical fraternity encourages him in this practice. Then the historian synthesizes the material obtained from all sources, provides his own interpretive structure based on the facts, and thereby produces a secondary work.

All textbooks and monographs are secondary works. So are collections of primary materials if they have been substantively edited or interpreted by their author. In fact, any primary material that has been altered in content becomes a secondary work. It is with these secondary works that the beginning history student will develop his greatest acquaintance and use.

C. *Journal Articles*   The beginning history student will also probably use some journal articles. These, too, are secondary-type materials, but they are much shorter in length than books. They contain much practical information, and there are two decided advantages associated with the use of journal articles, depending upon the form. For one, articles in professional historical journals yield a great deal of oftentimes not readily accessible fact, because these articles are quite detailed.[1] For another point, articles in newspapers and popular magazines offer the advantages of popularly written language, clear and concise meaning, and usually a very interesting format. The major disadvantage of the professional historical journal article is often a highly pedantic style, which, although readily understood by the professional historian, is quite often imagined to be dull and boring to the novice historian (once a real interest in history is developed, however, this attitude will disappear). A major disadvantage of articles in newspapers and magazines is the questionability of some of the fact, plus a great deal of interpretation in many such articles.[2]

2. TYPES OF STUDENT HISTORICAL WRITING

The above are the types of historical writings that the student will rely on for basic fact and information. But they do not constitute the types of writing that he will be called upon to produce as class assignments. These are five basic types of historical writing forms which the beginning student may be required to utilize for his class assignments. These forms apply to most courses other than history as well. They are: book reviews, book reports, journal article reviews, journal article reports, and the term paper.

The student should be thoroughly familiar with the differences among these various writing forms. As far as their exact styling is concerned some colleges and universities have published their own

[1] The bibliography contains a representative list of some of the major historical journals.

[2] The problem of reliability of newspaper articles is handled very well in Allan Nevins, *Gateway to History* (rev. ed.; Boston: D. C. Heath and Company, 1962).

style sheets. If the institution does not have an established style, individual instructors sometimes develop their own format. Because of the possibility of this, what follows is simply the description of the content and approaches of these various writing forms. However, in the absence of special instructions to the contrary, the student would be safe in following the suggestions and guidelines indicated below.

A. *Book Reviews*   A book review is a critical analysis of a book, preceded by a full bibliographical citation of the work being reviewed.[3] It does not summarize the contents of the book. Rather, it is an evaluation of the technique, organization, and thesis of the author as it is contained in the work. Book reviews are quite extensively used in professional journal publications because they give the reader a short, concise account of the type of material found in the work. Widely known fact within the book receives little or no attention, and the reviewer concentrates on evaluating what is new or different in it. The competent book reviewer requires a fairly thorough knowledge both of the subject area with which the book deals and of all related literature. For this reason the book review is usually quite difficult for the beginning student. It is sometimes preferred by the instructor, however, because it demonstrates knowledge and understanding in a very short paper and requires a considerable amount of thought and planning.

B. *Book Reports*   Book reports are a customary type of assignment for lower division history students. A book report is a summary of the contents, plot, or thesis of a particular book, again, preceded by a full bibliographical citation. The writer of a book report is not required to evaluate the author, although he often does so. He is usually content to summarize the contents of the work. Book reports will vary in length, depending on the individual preferences of the instructor. Usually, however, a book report is limited to two or three double-spaced typewritten pages. A book report indicates whether the student has read the book and whether or not he understands sufficiently what he has read. It is one of the easiest assignments the student will receive.

C. *Journal Article Reviews*   A journal article review, paralleling the book review, is a critical analysis of the work under consideration. The only real difference is that the work being reviewed is an article in a periodical rather than a full-length book. Otherwise the procedure and contents are the same. However, a journal article review is

[3] Consult the bibliographical citations contained in Appendix A for examples of style and sequence.

more often than not much shorter than a book review—it is usually limited to one page or less. A decided advantage of the journal article review is that a number of such reviews can be assigned without overburdening the student, and this consequently introduces the student to a broader range of materials and authors.

D. *Journal Article Reports*   A journal article report is very similar to a book report in that it is primarily a summary of an article. It does not usually contain an evaluation. Journal article reports are often a favored assignment of the history instructor because the student is capable of writing quite a number of them in the same length of time required to handle one book report. Consequently, as is the case with the journal article review, the student is given a greater breadth of historical materials, receives a wider acquaintanceship with writers of history, and becomes familiar with the various historical journals.

E. *The Term Paper* [4]   By far the most difficult writing assignment (and research assignment as well) that the student will encounter is the term paper. In order to write a term paper in history he must read a number of secondary works and journal articles on a particular topic, and then integrate the information acquired from these sources into his own ordering and interpretation of the topic.

The thesis that is presented, i.e., the interpretive structure being given to the facts, need not be that of the student. He is perfectly free to use the ideas and points of view found in the works that he has read. But he must, under all circumstances, cite the sources of his information, giving full credit whenever it is due. The student should never quote from works or make use of the ideas of other writers without informing his reader. Otherwise, he would be guilty of the extremely serious offense of plagiarism—a form of cheating.

Consequently, in order to attain complete intellectual honesty in the use of material, the term paper should be footnoted. And because footnoting is both very important and very complex the next section is devoted to it. The term paper should also contain a bibliography, i. e., a properly cited list of all the materials that were consulted in the writing of the paper, whether they were actually utilized or not.

The length of the term paper will vary, again depending on the individual preferences of the instructor. If no guidelines are prescribed, ten to fifteen typewritten pages, double spaced, would usually constitute an adequate length for the body of the paper. It should be

[4] For a very detailed consideration on the nature of historical writing, see Sherman Kent, *Writing History* (2nd ed.; New York: Appleton-Century-Crofts, Inc., 1967), available in paperback.

preceded by a title page and a table of contents and completed with the bibliography.

The term paper is an excellent exercise in historical method, for not only must the student seek out and evaluate his materials, thereby gaining good library experience and basic research technique, but also he is forced to integrate his material in a logical fashion and supply continuity to his presentation. Coupled with this, the term paper provides an excellent exercise in the mechanics of historical writing, i.e., the footnote usage and bibliographical citation mentioned above. And finally, the term paper provides good training in historical reading—historians are rapid, voluminous readers, and this is an attribute which comes only through long practice.

Choosing a topic   Great care should be exercised in selecting a topic for a term paper. First of all, the student should decide upon a topic that, if at all possible, is of considerable interest to himself. He will be working with it for some time, and if he does not find it personally interesting, a potentially satisfying task will turn into an unpleasant chore. Second, the student must ascertain whether or not adequate materials are available on the subject in which he is interested. He should begin by going to the various reference works listed in the bibliography at the end of this book. These reference works will guide him to the necessary literature for his topic. Third, he should check his reference list against the library card catalog in order to determine the availability of a sufficient number of pertinent works to provide him with enough information to write his paper. Many a student has spent dozens of hours working on a particular topic and then discovered that sufficient materials were unavailable. Proper preliminary research can prevent this from happening.

In checking the library for materials the student should always carefully fill out a bibliography card for each pertinent work that he locates. This procedure has a twofold purpose. On the one hand it will eventually prove to be a timesaver by avoiding the necessity of rechecking the library later if it is decided that a particular work is going to be used in writing the term paper. On the other hand the student will already have in his possession all of the necessary information for a full bibliographical entry at the end of his paper or for a footnote citation in the text.

For the bibliography card, a standard 3″ × 5″ index card is recommended, but any uniform card or sheet is satisfactory provided only that it is not so large as to prove unwieldy and that it is durable (the card will be handled a great deal). The student should be very careful to avoid placing more than one bibliographical citation on each card; otherwise, he may run into organizational difficulties later on in his research.

At the lower left (there is no set rule, just tradition) should be placed the library call number. This is to be done strictly for the convenience of the student. It will avoid the possible necessity of having to recheck the library card catalog at a later date for the same work. It is a simple little procedure, but it will save considerable time and effort. And it should be pointed out that some professors may require the catalog number as part of the bibliographical entry.

The bibliography card takes the following form:

Kurtz, Stephen G. *The Presidency of John Adams.* Philadelphia: The University of Pennsylvania Press, 1957.

Cat. #

Note that the last name of the author appears first (as in the library card catalog), followed by the first name and middle initial, followed by a period. The complete title of the work comes next, again followed by a period. Underlining (italicizing) the title on the bibliography card is optional. After the title are placed all of the pertinent facts of publication, such as the number of volumes, edition of the work, revision, editor, or translator. Then comes the location of publication, followed by a colon, the name of the publisher, followed by a comma, and finally, the copyright date or date of publication, followed by a period.

The form used in filling out a bibliography card as explained and illustrated above is the same for a bibliographical citation with two minor exceptions: one, the library catalog number is usually not included in the bibliographical citation, and two, the title of any work should always be underlined (the form used to indicate italics) wherever it appears in the paper, whereas it is not necessary to underline it on a bibliography card. Possible error can be avoided by getting into the habit of underlining all titles, whether necessary or not, as was done in the illustration (indicated by italics).

Also, in the bibliographical entry it is often the practice to annotate the entry, i.e., to indicate in a few short phrases or a sentence the particular usefulness of that work. An annotated bibliography is usually far more meaningful and informative to the reader than a straight bibliographical entry. Examples of this technique are to be found in Appendix A at the end of this work. One suggestion: if the student plans to annotate his bibliography (and the instructor might make this a requirement), it would be a good idea to jot down appropriate comments on the back of the bibliography card immediately after reading the work, lest, by the time the bibliography is being written, perhaps two months later, part of the impressions and utility of the work might be forgotten.

Note taking   Having selected a topic and having determined the availability of materials, the writer of the term paper is now ready to begin the acquisition of information. It is time to begin reading the selected works and to take notes on them properly. The taking of proper notes is extremely important. It can result in the saving of tremendous amounts of time, and it can lessen the possibility of factual error in the term paper.

Students quite often experience considerable difficulty in taking notes properly. They usually fall into one of two categories: Either they take notes far too profusely, or they take them far too sparsely. It is safe to state that it would be better to take too many notes than too few, but such a procedure would be a waste of time and effort. It would definitely be better to use the additional time and effort to learn the techniques of proper note-taking.

Students at the lower division level who take their notes too profusely are either afraid that they might be missing something, or, and this is more often the reason, they are not really certain about what they are going to write. Consequently they are not really sure what to look for in their reading. This is oftentimes the result of not having selected a topic carefully. There is no single answer to this difficulty; however, simple guidelines can be suggested.

Always remember that notes are to be taken only on what is really important or complex and only if they aid in understanding a particular viewpoint. Paragraphs or pages should normally not be copied from a secondary work verbatim. The experienced notetaker summarizes the material *in his own words,* for this is an excellent personal test of his understanding of what he has just read (it is also a good practice for everyday studying, incidentally). Notes pertaining to different ideas and topics, or coming from different works, should always be written on separate sheets usually a 5″ × 7″ size, including the page number or numbers on which the material was located. Thus, if the note is actually used in writing the term paper the writer will have all necessary information for a footnote citation in his possession. Above all else, the student should always avoid taking notes continuously on sheets of paper as if he were taking down notes in a lecture or studying from the course textbook. Notes written in this continuous manner are of practically no use in organizing and writing a term paper. Cardinal rule number one: Notes should always be taken in the notetaker's own words, with no more than one idea or topic being placed on a single note card.

It cannot be emphasized enough that the student should avoid taking notes in the exact words of the author whom he is reading, unless a particular statement lends considerable support to the term paper thesis or is extremely succinct. The term paper should not consist of page upon page of long, direct quotations from some text, occasionally linked together by a sentence or two written by the student (some papers, by the very nature of the topic, however, will require considerably more direct quotation than other papers). The history instructor is interested in determining whether or not the student has successfully integrated and developed materials taken from a variety of sources.

But on the other hand, it is not prudent to be parsimonious in the taking of notes. If the student should happen to come upon a strong idea, one which concisely supports a portion of his paper, it would be a good idea to copy pertinent portions of it verbatim on a note card, provided that the student believes that there is a distinct possibility that he will quote the material directly in his term paper. This procedure will avoid the possible necessity of being required to re-check the work later. But the student should not get upset by the fact that in the actual writing of the paper he may not make use of every tiny note taken during his reading. Students have a tendency of forcing material into a paper whether it belongs there or not, just because they have the material on a note card. Only a fraction of notes taken will actually be used in the paper.

Always remember that when one copies material verbatim, it should be edited. Sentences or phrases that are not pertinent should be deleted. This is done by inserting three successive dots between quoted materials. The dots indicate to the reader that something has been omitted. If an entire paragraph is being omitted, this should be indicated by a line of asterisks. If the writer adds words to quoted material in order to bridge or explain omitted sections, this is indicated by enclosing his additions in brackets. And to avoid confusion, always place quotation marks around material that is taken down verbatim.

The student should be very careful to indicate exact pagination of quoted materials on his note cards, especially if the materials span more than a single page. Indicate on the note card exactly where the quote changes from one page to the next. Again, this might save time later on, for in the actual writing of the paper, the student may discover that he only wants to quote a portion of the material, and he will know thereby exactly where it appeared. Cardinal rule number two: The student should copy pertinent material verbatim only when he feels that there is a strong probability that he will use the material verbatim in his term paper, although he should not feel obligated to do so.

By way of a final observation, as stated before, if the student is going to take his notes properly, he must have a clear idea what he is going to write. This reflects the thoroughness of his initial research and thought in choosing a topic. Therefore, Cardinal rule number three: The student should know exactly what he is looking for before he begins his detailed reading. When he finds what he is looking for, then, and only then, should he take notes on it.

Once the reading has been completed, the student should then categorize all note cards from all sources according to date, topic, person, or some other mode of classification that corresponds to the proposed organization of the term paper. If a chronological organization is intended, categorize notes according to date. If a topical approach is anticipated, categorize by event. No matter what approach is utilized, the student will thus accumulate stacks of note cards which will apply to a given chapter or other unit within the term paper. This is one very good method of integrating the various materials consulted in researching the term paper topic.

Experienced students develop more sophisticated techniques for categorizing notes. Some use different colored cards for different categories. Others use key punch cards, punching out a certain slot for a certain topic. All cards are then placed in a box with a coded card in the front indicating which slot represents which topic. A knitting needle, or some similar device, is inserted through the stack and raised. All cards pertaining to a given topic will then fall out of the stack. There are various commercial devices, which are based on this technique, now available. The student who plans a career in history might do well to check into these laborsaving devices.

When the instructor commences the reading of a term paper and discovers that only one work is cited repeatedly for the first half-dozen pages, then a different work only is cited for the next half-dozen pages, and so forth, he immediately suspects, with considerable justification, that the student has not taken good notes and has not organized his notes properly. It becomes evident to the instructor that the student has not successfully integrated his materials, and this, of course, is one of the most important purposes for a term paper assignment. Only by correct note-taking procedure is the student able to properly organize and integrate his various materials. One final note: Never underestimate your instructor. He is a trained historian, and it is fairly easy for him to determine whether or not a student has proceeded properly in a term paper assignment.

From what has been said, it would seem that writing a term paper is a rather difficult task. It is, but if the student proceeds with a positive attitude and has chosen a topic in which he is really interested, it can be a rather pleasant and rewarding task. A great deal of satisfaction can be derived from constructing such a paper.

It is hoped that the aforementioned suggestions on note-taking will guide the student in organizing and writing a better term paper. But what has already been stated is not quite enough information for writing a good term paper in a history class. The student must also be able to document his material accurately and according to accepted procedures. He must know the mechanics of good historical writing.

Proper footnoting technique is probably one of the most difficult procedures for the student to master. But although it is a difficult task, fortunately there exists a fairly well-accepted set of rules that govern footnote citation.

3. TYPES AND USE OF FOOTNOTES

Foonotes may be of two types: reference and content. Reference footnotes are used either to cite an authority for statements, quotations, or ideas presented in the text, or to refer to materials and authorities already cited previously in the text. Content footnotes provide elaboration on material found in the body of the text which is somewhat tangental and might destroy continuity, but which at the same time is somewhat interesting and relevant. A content footnote may also be employed to acknowledge some individual or work which is not actually being used in the work, but which contains useful information on the same subject.[5]

Footnoting should be performed both systematically and discriminately. First of all, let us consider the system employed. Footnotes should be assigned arabic numbers in ascending order, i.e., 2, 3, 4, 5, etc., beginning anew on each page, beginning anew with each chapter (the method employed in the work you are now reading), or running continuously throughout the entire work. No number should ever be skipped. If a footnote is deleted during the course of writing a paper, all subsequent footnotes must be renumbered accordingly. This is one good reason for using the chapter numbering technique rather than numbering through the entire work—it saves a great deal of effort if a footnote is deleted.

In the body of the text the arabic number should immediately follow the material being footnoted, and it should be placed approximately one-half line above the line of the textual material in the very

---

[5] All of the preceding footnotes contained in this work would fit into this category. They simply refer the reader to particularly good works for further reading and elaboration. This note, incidentally, is strictly a content footnote.

next space following punctuation marks, if any. Note the following illustrations.

> ". . . and as result the war came to an end." [3]
> "I have but one life to give for my country." [4]
> There is no real basis for this idea,[5] but we should . . .

Bear in mind that the arabic number is to be placed at the end of the material being quoted or acknowledged if it is a reference footnote (the first two examples above). It may possibly be placed near the beginning or even in the middle of a sentence if it is a content footnote (third example above). As is the case with the reference footnote, the content footnote should be placed as closely as possible to the material to which it refers, provided only that it does not destroy the continuity of the sentence. Good discretionary judgment should prevail.

Every footnote number found in the text of a page must also have its counterpart at the foot of the same page (an exceptionally long footnote may begin on one page and carry over to the foot of the next page, but this rarely happens). Proper spacing must be allowed for footnotes in the typing of the paper. At the bottom of the page the same footnote number that is found in the body of the text is to be placed immediately preceding the footnote material, and it is to be raised approximately one-half line above it, with no spacing between the number and the footnote material. The first line of a footnote should be indented in the same manner as a paragraph in the text. Subsequent lines should be single spaced, whereas all material in the body of the text should be double spaced. In published works the footnote type is smaller than the type used in the text. The above procedure is simply the typist's way of indicating the same delineation. Note the following examples of footnote citation, paying especial heed to spacing.

[13] Patrick Gardiner, *Theories of History* (Glencoe, Illinois: The Free Press, 1959), p. —.

[14] John Bury, *The Idea of Progress* (London: Macmillan and Company, Ltd., 1921), p. —.

A reference footnote must contain the following information in the exact order as it is listed (refer to the preceding examples): full name of the author, complete title of the work, all facts of publication, and the exact location in the work from which the material is being extracted. Let us now consider each of these units of footnote information in detail, indicating proper punctuation.

A. *Name* The complete name of the author in its normal form is indicated first. It is followed by a comma. No titles such as Mr., Dr., or Professor are to be used. It should be pointed out that an author may be an institution, committee, or agency as well as an individual. The same format prevails, however, as for the individual. Examples of authors who are other than individuals are: United States, Office of Education; United States Senate, Committee on the Judiciary; American Federation of Labor; and Metropolitan Church Federation.

Some works have more than one author. If there are three authors or fewer, list every one of them according to the procedure already outlined. If there are more than three authors, list only the name of the first author appearing on the title page of the work, followed by the underlined (italicized) words "*et al.,*" the Latin abbreviation which means "and others." If the work is a compilation or anthology, list only the name of the principal editor, followed by the abbreviation (ed.) in parentheses as indicated, followed by a comma. Note the following examples of author citation.

Karl Lowith. [One author only]
United States Senate, Committee on the Judiciary. [Author is an agency or institution]
Oscar T. Barck and Nelson M. Blake. [Three or fewer authors]
Wood Gray, *et al.* [More than three authors]
Robert Maynard Hutchins (ed.). [An editor of a work]

Occasionally works that do not have a known author may be consulted. Two procedures may be employed under these circumstances. One is simply to ignore the name of the author and begin the footnote citation with the exact title, followed by the facts of publication, and so on. When this procedure is used it is assumed that the reader will understand that there is not a known author for the work. The assumption is not quite valid, because there are some works that have no author (refer to the citations in the bibliography for examples of this). Hence, the reader does not know if there is no author or no known author—this constitutes quite a difference. The other technique is more concise. Use the term *"non auctoris"* in lieu of the author's name. The term literally means "no author," but it is widely understood to mean that there is an author for the work but that his name is not known.

B. *Title* The title of the book or other type of publication is next cited exactly as it appears on the title page. Even if the spelling, capitalization, or punctuation are incorrect in the title, it is to be listed exactly as it appears. The insertion of the abbreviation *"sic."* in brackets indicates to the reader that the error is not that of the writer of the paper but the error of the author or publisher, or both. The only exception to the rule indicated occurs when the work in question carries a subtitle. In this instance the main title is to be listed, followed by the subtitle, but with a colon inserted between the two titles (added punctuation). The entire title should always be underlined (i.e., it should be italicized, and this is indicated by underlining it).

If the title is that of an article within a periodical, the title of the article should be placed within quotation marks, followed by the title of the periodical itself. Only the periodical title should be underlined. The article title and the periodical title should be separated by a comma. Study the following illustrations carefully.

[1] Karl Lowith, *Meaning in History*. [An example of an exact title of a book]

[2] Oscar T. Barck and Nelson M. Blake, *Since 1900: A History of the United States in Our Times*. [A book with a subtitle and added punctuation (the colon)]

[3] Julius W. Pratt, "The Origins of Manifest Destiny," *American Historical Review*. [An article within a periodical with proper punctuation]

The first line of a footnote, it should be recalled, must be indented in the same manner as a paragraph. The second and succeeding lines of a footnote begin at the margin and are single spaced. Again, note the illustrations above.

Following the title there may be a reference to the compiler or editor of the work. This can be a little confusing, especially since an editor's name can also precede the work. But certain rules govern its placement. If one author is writing about the works of another author and quoting his material extensively, or if he is collecting various materials from numerous authors, as in an anthology, his name precedes the work followed by (ed.), as already indicated. However, if he is composing a new edition of an already existing work by a different author, the other author's name comes first, followed by the title of the work, followed by the author of the new edition, preceded by the abbreviation "ed." which is *not* placed in parenthesis.

C. *Facts of publication* Following this sometimes confusing point, we next move to the facts of publication. All of the facts of publication pertaining to a work are set off by parentheses in the footnote (but not in the bibliography). The opening of the parentheses comes either immediately after the title with no intervening punctuation, or after the name of the editor, if an editor's name follows the title, again, with no intervening punctuation.

The facts of publication include, first of all, the number of volumes in the work. The number of volumes is indicated only if the work consists of more than a single volume. If no indication of volumes is given in the reference, the reader may safely assume that the work is a single-volume work. The number of volumes is always indicated by an arabic number, followed by the abbreviation "vols." Examples are: 4 vols., 13 vols., etc. Never capitalize the abbreviated version of "volumes" in a footnote citation pertaining to the facts of publication.

After the number of volumes, if any, comes the edition number of the work. If no edition is indicated, the reader may safely assume that the work is a first edition. The edition of the work is expressed according to the following illustrations: rev. ed., 2nd ed., 4th ed., and 6th ed. This information is shown on the title page of the work. Do not confuse it with the number of printings, which may also be indicated. A suggestion that will avoid confusion is to refer to the latest edition and copyright date indicated. Each edition has to be copyrighted separately, because technically it is a different work. Although all copyright dates may be indicated in the work, always use only the most recent one.

It will quite often happen that neither one of these first two facts of publication will be applicable to most works. But the other facts of publication will always be applicable to all works. If only one of these first two facts is cited, it is to be followed with a semicolon. If both of them should happen to be applicable, separate them with a comma and follow the second fact with a semicolon.

The next fact of publication is concerned with the place where the work was published. Note that this refers to the location of publication, not of writing. Simply indicate the city where it was published. This information may be obtained from the title page of the work. If the title page makes mention of several cities, cite only the name of the first one to appear. If the city listed is not one that would be immediately known to most readers, include either the state or the nation, whichever is most appropriate, separated by a comma. The place of publication is to be followed by a colon.

The complete name of the publishing company, as found on the title page, follows the colon. Many historians do not list the publishing company in their citations, and some history departments do likewise by established policy. If the student chooses to omit the citation in the footnote, he should place it in the bibliography. Follow the preferences of the instructor making the assignment.

After the name of the publishing company, if it is being indicated, place a comma followed by the copyright date alluded to above. If more than one copyright date is listed, use only the most recent. If no copyright date is indicated in the work, this fact can be made known to the reader by the symbol "n. d.," which stands for "no date indicated." If the copyright date is determined from some source other than the work itself, it should be indicated, but not in the normal form. Simply place it in brackets. If the work was written over a period of years, indicate such information according to the following procedure: 1952–1957, 1817–1842, or 1968–1969. And if it is a multi-volumed work that is still in the process of being written and published, but which has already witnessed the publication of some of its volumes, write 1966–. The dash indicates that the total work is not yet completed and that other volumes are to appear at a later date. Relevant examples of this form are to be found in the bibliography.

The date concludes the facts of publication. This should be indicated by closing the parentheses and adding a period. For example:

[15] Donald Sheehan, *The Making of American History* (2 vols., rev. ed.; New York: The Dryden Press, 1954).

D. *Location of referenced material*　The last portion of the reference footnote citation concerns the exact portion of the work from which the material footnoted is being drawn or quoted. If the work is a multi-volumed work, first list the volume number. This is designated by a roman numeral, e.g., II, III, IV. No mention of the word "volume" is necessary; this has been taken care of in the facts of publication. Also, note that the number of volumes in the facts of publication is designated by an arabic number. The reason for this switch in number forms will become evident in a moment.

Follow the volume number with a comma and add the page number. If one page is being referred to, write "p. 17." If several continuous pages are being referred to, write "pp. 17–22." If two or more different pages, which are not continuous, are being referred to, write "pp. 45 and 51." This, however, is only done when the same idea is being expressed in various parts of the work. Separate ideas and separate quotations must be cited separately. Now we can explain the reason for the roman numeral being used to express the volume number in the citation. It would be rather confusing to write "4, p. 4" There is considerable possibility of error (or at the very least the reader would be required to reread it) on the part of the reader. Less susceptible to error would be "IV, p. 4."

There is only one exception to the volume number procedure as outlined above. This has to do with reference to articles that appear in periodicals. Instead of the volume number appearing after the facts of publication, it comes immediately after the title of the periodical. The reason for this is that there are no such facts of publication applying to periodicals as they do toward books. The volume number of a periodical follows the periodical title, preceded by a comma, as follows: "XXVI." It is followed by the year and the month of publication (certain periodicals might require the exact date, e.g., newspapers), and these are enclosed by parentheses and followed by a comma. Last comes the citing of the page number. This requires no elaborate comment; it is identical in form to that of the book citation. The edition, location and name of the publisher, and the number of volumes of the periodical as a fact of publication, do not apply to periodical citations. Note the difference between a book citation and a periodical citation in the following illustration.

¹ Thomas A. Bailey, *A Diplomatic History of the American People* (4th ed.; New York: Appleton-Century-Crofts, Inc., 1950), p. —.

² G. B. Adams, "History and the Philosophy of History," *American Historical Review*, XIV (1909), p. 769.

Mention should also be made of the proper form for citing those government documents that are frequently utilized by historians. The most frequently used documents are court decisions, the citing of laws, and proceedings contained in the official congressional publications.

A Supreme Court case is cited according to the following sequence: name of the case, information on where the case can be located, and date of the decision. For example, *Hepburn v. Griswold*, 8 Wallace 603 (February 7, 1870), is a complete Supreme Court citation. *Hepburn v. Griswold* is the name or title of the case. It should always be underlined (italicized) and followed by a comma. The location of the case information is a bit more complex and will be taken up momentarily. It is followed by the date on which the Court actually rendered its decision. This date should be enclosed in parentheses, and normally the year of the decision is sufficient. Occasionally, however, it might be necessary to cite the month and day of the decision.

With regard to the location of case information, "8 Wallace 603" means that the decision may be found in volume 8, page 603, of the Court Reports during the period when a man named Wallace was the Clerk of the Court. Thus, many different names will appear, e.g., Peters, Howard, and Wheaton, until late in 1875 when a new procedure was adopted. From that time on, the name of the clerk was dropped, and in its place is used the simple term "U. S.," which stands for United States Supreme Court Reports. An example of this would be: *Tot v. United States*, 319 U. S. 463 (June 7, 1943).

The citing of decisions from other types of courts is handled in about the same manner. Only the location of the case information will vary. And since there are so many variations of this (literally hundreds), the student should consult specialized guides in political science for guidelines, should the need arise.

The procedure for citing federal laws is quite simple. Such material is cited according to the following form: 46 *Stat.* 21 (1929). This signifies that the law will be found in volume 46 of the *United States Statutes*, beginning on page 21, and was passed in 1929. Other legislative bodies follow a similar pattern. However, the variances are so many that what holds for the citing of non-Supreme Court cases also holds true here.

Materials recording congressional proceedings that are not laws follow the same general form used to cite a federal law. There are only two exceptions to this: (1) *United States Statutes* is replaced by an abbreviated form of *Congressional Record, Congressional Globe,* etc., and (2) any additional information that will more accurately direct the reader to the source should be included. Note the following two illustrations.

⁴ 88 *Congressional Record* 7044, 77th Cong., 2nd sess. (September 7, 1942).

⁵ 81 *Congressional Record,* Part V, 5639, Senate Report No. 711 (June 14, 1937).

For the minute details of citation, and for unusual or rarely used citation material, the reader is referred to one of the several excellent advanced guides available.⁶

For the benefit of the reader, sample illustrations of the various rules indicated above are presented below. While reading them pay special attention to the placement of punctuation marks and the sequence of citation material. All of the materials listed constitute excellent sources for further study in history (depending on personal interests, of course), and they are highly recommended. Page and volume numbers are included for illustration purposes only, except for journal articles and government documents. They do not refer to any particular item on the page, nor has any material been quoted from these works. The manner in which the footnotes are listed, incidentally, is widely acceptable. Footnotes may be cited at the foot of each page as they occur, or they may be collected at the end of each

---

⁶ One of the best works is: Kate L. Turabian, *A Manual for Writers of Term Papers, Theses, and Dissertations* (rev. ed.; Chicago: The University of Chicago Press, 1955).

chapter, or at the end of the entire work. Follow the preference of your instructor.

[1] Arnold Toynbee, *A Study of History* (12 vols.; New York: Oxford University Press, 1934–1961), VIII, p. 831.

[2] Elmer Ellis, "The Profession of Historian," *Mississippi Valley Historical Review*, XXXVIII (1951), pp. 3–20. [Illustrations of periodical citations list correct volume numbers. The pages refer to the exact pages within the periodical concerning the article.]

[3] Michael Kraus, *The Writing of American History* (Norman: The University of Oklahoma Press, 1953), p. 350.

[4] *Corporation of Brick Church v. Mayor, et al.*, 5 Cowen (N. Y.) 538 (1826). [This is an example of a state court decision citation.]

[5] A. L. Rowse, *The Expansion of Elizabethan England* (London: Macmillan and Company, Ltd., 1955), p. 700.

[6] Worthington C. Ford and Gaillard Hunt (eds.), *The Journals of the Continental Congress* (34 vols.; Washington: Government Printing Office, 1904–07), XIII, p. 67.

[7] Hiram M. Chittenden, *The American Fur Trade of the Far West* (2 vols.; New York: The Press of the Pioneers, Inc., 1935), I, p. 789.

[8] Francis Parkman, *France and England in North America*, ed. Samuel E. Morison (London: Faber and Faber, 1956), p. 999.

[9] F. Lee Benns, *Europe Since 1914: In Its World Setting* (8th ed.; New York: Appleton-Century-Crofts, Inc., 1954), p. 53.

[10] 37 *Stat.* 699 (1913). [This is a federal law citation.]

[11] Board of Governors of the Federal Reserve System, *The Federal Reserve System: Purposes and Functions* (5th ed.; Washington: Division of Administrative Services, Board of Governors of the Federal Reserve System, 1964), p. 78.

[12] Ross M. Robertson, *History of the American Economy* (2nd ed.; New York: Harcourt, Brace & World, 1964), p. 566.

[13] *Muskrat v. United States*, 219 U. S. 346 (1911).

[14] Meribeth Cameron, Thomas Mahoney, and George McReynolds, *China, Japan and the Powers* (2nd ed; New York: The Ronald Press, 1960), p. 555.

[15] United States, *Congressional Record*, Vol. LXXXI, Part V, Senate Report No. 777, p. 5639. [The reader is cautioned of the fact that government document references fit no exact pattern. Record all pertinent information starting from the most general and working toward the particular.]

[16] Herman Ausubel, *et al.* (eds.), *Some Modern Historians of Britain* (New York: The Dryden Press, 1951), p. 600.

[17] *Ware v. Hylton*, 3 Dallas 199 (1797).

[18] New York *Evening Post*, March 15, 1862, p. 7. [For newspaper citations simply list the name of the paper with the city of publication

if not in the name, the date, and the volume number if available. Underline the official title of the paper.]

[19] William T. Hutchinson, "The American Historian in Wartime," *Mississippi Valley Historical Review*, XXIX (September, 1942), pp. 163–186. [Occasionally periodicals are bound into volumes which do not correspond to the volume numbers of the periodical. Inclusion of the date is consequently quite important.]

[20] Elliott Roosevelt (ed.), *FDR: His Personal Letters 1928–1945* (2 vols.; New York: Duell, Sloan and Pearce, 1950), II, p. 900.

E. *The Content Footnote*   The content footnote possesses no set style. It is strictly an information-type note written in textual form. It is numbered in exactly the same manner as is the reference footnote. All footnotes are numbered continuously whether they are reference or content or, as is usually the case, a combination of the two. Spacing and indentation are identical. The only difference is that instead of a citation, the content footnote contains subject matter, usually to the extent of a very short paragraph but occasionally consisting of only a brief sentence. A few samples of content footnotes appear on the illustration pages that follow at the end of this chapter.

There is one variation of the use of the content footnote. This is used to refer the reader to another section or page within the work. It is technically known as the cross-reference footnote. Most frequently the cross-reference footnote is written as follows: [4] *Supra*, p. 67., or [4] *Infra*, p. 67., meaning that the reader is referred to p. 67 of the work for a further elaboration or review of similar type material. *Supra* translates as "above," and *Infra* translates as "below." Some writers prefer to use the terms "above" and "below" instead of their Latin forms, or even to write a sentence in the footnote explaining the cross reference. All of these forms are acceptable, but once the writer has used one of them, he should not use any other form within that particular work. The various forms should not be intermingled.

Caution and sound thought should always be employed in footnoting. Unfortunately, some students suffer from an uncontrollable tendency to overload their papers with footnotes, believing that the papers will consequently appear quite scholarly. However, a heavily footnoted paper does not necessarily reflect solid scholarship. A rule that should always be followed is this: Never footnote unless necessary for acknowledgement or clarity. The ability to footnote, in itself, does not necessarily make either a good historian or a good student of history. Good judgment in footnoting is a far more important ingredient.

By this time the reader is probably ready to breathe a sigh of relief in that he believes the footnote discussion has now come to an end. Unfortunately, such is not the case. The procedure outlined above concerning the styling of reference footnotes applies only to initial references to a particular work. Later references to previously cited works may be shortened in a variety of ways. The student should always bear in mind, however, that he must remain with whatever method of shortening he initially chooses to follow; the various methods are not interchangeable within a given work. And it should be pointed out that it is not necessary to shorten later references to previously cited works. The initial procedure may very properly be repeated throughout the paper. However, when there is a simpler and shorter way of doing something, why not use it?

The simplest, and a perfectly acceptable, method is to cite later reference to a work in an abbreviated fashion. When this method is used the exact mode of abbreviation should be indicated in the first full reference to the work, lest the reader be confused. The following first reference footnote gives an illustration as to how this should be done.

[18] Gilbert J. Garraghan, *A Guide to Historical Method*, ed. Jean Delanglez (New York: Fordham University Press, 1946), p. —. Hereafter cited as Garraghan, *Guide*.

This indicates to the reader that all future references to the work will be cited only as Garraghan, *Guide*, plus the appropriate page number. It should be borne in mind that when this method is employed, no other method may be used. The principal advantages are: one, it is very simple to use, and two, it is very easy to follow.

A more scholarly technique is to use the Latin abbreviations *ibid.*, *op. cit.*, and *loc. cit.* when referring to the works that have been previously cited in full form. This, of course, presupposes the fact that these abbreviations are used in the correct manner.

The term *"ibid."* is the abbreviation for *Ibidem*, meaning "in the same place." It is used only under two conditions.

1. In a reference to an article within a periodical, the term *ibid.* may be used to refer to the title of the periodical if another article from the same periodical is quoted in the very next footnote. Note the following example.

[7] Rush Welter, "The History of Ideas in America: An Essay in Redefinition," *The Journal of American History*, LI (March, 1965), p. 599.

[8] John W. Caughey, "Our Chosen Destiny," *Ibid.*, LII (September, 1965), p. 239.

The *ibid.* in the second footnote above refers to *The Journal of American History*. It could not have been used if an intervening footnote, referring to another periodical or book, had been present. It cannot refer to an author or title within a periodical itself. Remember that *ibid.* means "in the same place," i.e., the periodical, not the same work, which would refer to the article itself.

2. When no intervening reference occurs between a first full citation and the next reference to the same work, the footnote or footnotes may read *ibid.* The *ibid.* in this case stands for the name of the author, the title of the work, and the facts of publication. Note the following set of examples.

[5] Ray Billington, *Westward Expansion: A History of the American Frontier* (New York: The Macmillan Company, 1949), p. 113.
[6] *Ibid.*, p. 641.
[7] *Ibid.*, p. 532.

This is correct. The second two footnotes above refer to different page numbers in *Westward Expansion,* and there has been no intervening reference to a different work.

If the writer chooses to use *ibid.*, he may also use the abbreviation "*op. cit.*," which stands for *opere citato,* meaning "in the work cited." Whenever *ibid.* cannot be used because of an intervening reference to a different work, the surname of the author, followed by *op. cit.*, should be used. For example:

[5] Frederick Allen, *The Big Change* (New York: Harper & Row, Publishers, 1952), p. 86.
[6] William Ebenstein, *Modern Political Thought* (2nd ed.; New York: Holt, Rinehart and Winston, Inc., 1960), p. 465.
[7] Allen, *op. cit.*, p. 204.

In the event that only one work by the same author is being cited in a paper, there is no problem with the use of *op. cit.* But it could happen that more than one work by the same author is being used. Under such circumstances *op. cit.* would not really indicate to the reader which work was being cited. Thus, the shortened form technique would have to be used in such an instance.

Besides *op. cit.*, the abbreviation "*loc. cit.*," standing for *loco citato,* "in the place cited," can be used under certain circumstances. If reference is being made to the *same page* and volume of a book or article previously cited, and intervening footnotes pertaining to different works have occurred thereby prohibiting the use of *ibid.*, the better abbreviation is *loc. cit.* rather than *op. cit.* This abbreviation is a little more specific than *op. cit.*, which refers only to a work in general. On the other hand, *loc. cit.* not only refers to a particular work but also stands for a specific place within that work. And obviously, under such a set of circumstances, no pagination is required in the footnote. It should be pointed out that *op. cit.* could be used in lieu of *loc. cit.*, but the volume number, if any, and the page number would have to be included.

Before proceeding to cite a list of different types of footnotes that illustrate all of the forms discussed, it would be well to caution the student in one respect: Footnotes are for the information of the reader. Whenever a work that has been fully cited is not referred to again for quite a number of pages, and a number of other various references have intervened, it would be a good idea to repeat the citation in full because in all probability the reader has forgotten the original citation. With this in mind, many authors prefer to treat each chapter as if it were a new work for footnote purposes. All references are cited in full the first time they are used in a chapter, even though they may have been cited a number of times in the preceding chapter. Utilization of this technique means that the reader will not be called upon to remember a particular complete citation for more than one chapter at the very most, and he will not be required to leaf back through the pages in search of the first full reference to the work in the event that he has forgotten it.

SAMPLE FOOTNOTE ILLUSTRATIONS

[1] Albert K. Weinberg, *Manifest Destiny* (Baltimore: The Johns Hopkins Press, 1935), p. 109.

[2] *Ibid.*, p. 112. This view is further developed in Richard Van Alstyne, "International Rivalries in the Pacific Northwest," *Oregon Historical Quarterly,* XLVI (1945).

[3] Norman Graebner, *Empire on the Pacific* (New York: The Ronald Press, 1955), p. 961.

[4] Weinberg, *op. cit.,* p. 27.

[5] *Smith v. Turner,* 7 Howard 283 (1849).

[6] Graebner, *op. cit.,* p. 92.

[7] William E. Dodd, "The West and the War with Mexico," *Journal of the Illinois State Historical Society,* V (1912), p. 222.

[8] Oscar O. Winther, *The Old Oregon Country* (Stanford: The Stanford University Press, 1950), p. 990.

[9] Allan Nevins, *Fremont, The West's Greatest Adventurer* (2 vols.; New York: Harper and Brothers, 1928), I, p. 138.

[10] *Ibid.*, II, p. 708.

[11] Weinberg, *op. cit.,* p. 233.

[12] *Supra,* p. 13, footnote number 7.

[13] Bernard De Voto, *The Year of Decision 1846* (Boston: Houghton Mifflin, 1942), p. 91.

[14] *Loc. cit.*

[15] 16 *Stat.* 341.

[16] But this is only one legitimate viewpoint on the subject. Some writers would feel, as was indicated in Chapter VII, that land hunger was a more important factor.

[17] De Voto, *op. cit.*, p. 121.

[18] Otis A. Singletary, *The Mexican War* (Chicago: The University of Chicago Press, 1960), p. 300.

[19] *Ibid.*, p. 394.

[20] *Ibid.*, p. 100.

[21] Nevins, *op. cit.*, II, p. 400.

[22] Singletary, *op. cit.*, p. 268.

[23] James T. Adams, *The Epic of America* (Boston: Little, Brown, 1931), p. 197. See also the works cited *Supra*, pp. 9, 17, 21, and 35.

Some writers and some publishers also prefer to list all footnotes at either the end of each chapter or by chapter at the end of the entire work, rather than to cite them at the foot of each page. If this method is utilized it would follow the exact pattern of the preceding illustration. Otherwise, it would be identical to the pattern used throughout the work you are now reading.

The technique of placing all footnotes at the end of the work is an acceptable one, and it does ease the burden of both typist and publisher, but it imposes a rather serious hardship on the reader, who is consequently required to page back and forth through the work if he desires to check footnote references. As a result, the footnotes in such works quite often go unheeded to all except the truly conscientious student and scholar.

AMERICAN HISTORIOGRAPHY

5

Whether making a selection for a book report or review, choosing works for inclusion in a term paper, or consulting works for an advanced research report, the student of history should possess a sound understanding and knowledge of the historiography of his field.

Historiography is the study of the various approaches to historical method, the actual writing of history, and, primarily, the various interpretations of historical events. Historiography is the study of the techniques employed by the individual historian. It is not necessary to study primary materials, i.e., original source materials, in order to study historiography. For historiography is concerned mainly with what has been written *about* historical events—the various schools of thought and interpretation centered around any particular historical occurrence—not with the source materials from which the historical fact was derived. The primary sources of historiography are the works of the historians themselves.

There are many significant controversial topics in American history. These topics possess numerous legitimate, and sometimes conflicting, interpretations. For as we pointed out near the beginning of this work, history is not an exact science. The historian will employ the scientific method up to a point, but he is forced to subject his scientifically acquired historical fact to a very fallible, nonscientific human interpretation.

History, especially American history, is often regarded as a "cut-and-dried" subject. In order to prove otherwise, here are some of the more controversial topics, those upon which historians are not agreed:

causes for the various American wars, the handling of post-Civil War reconstruction, the evaluation of progressive Republicanism, considerations on the importance of the New Deal, the significance of the so-called Jeffersonian revolution, the importance of Jacksonian democracy, the role of the capitalist in the development of an industrialized America, the significance of the frontier experience, and on and on and on. The list of major topics alone would be nearly impossible to exhaust, not to mention the multitudinous smaller events that have taken place during the history of the American nation.

Hence, this chapter is concerned with tracing in outline form the development of American historiography. The reader should bear in mind, however, that what follows is only a brief sketch. The study of American historiography is a deep and penetrating subject, requiring a thorough knowledge not only of historical fact but of individual American historians as well.

Fortunately, several highly competent historians have at various times published detailed studies on the development of the writing of American history. If the reader desires detailed information he can consult these works (and he is encouraged to do so).[1] Also, the various national professional historical journals such as the *American Historical Review*, the *Journal of American History* (successor to the old *Mississippi Valley Historical Review*), plus the many regional, state, and specialized journals contain considerable information on this type of material.[2] A brief selection of historiographical articles may be found in the Bibliography, Appendix A.

1. THE FOUNDATION PERIOD

In order to have the writing of an American history, a national consciousness had to be developed first. But the American nation, from the founding of Jamestown colony in 1607 to the close of the War of 1812 in December 1814, did not possess a true national consciousness. Consequently, the first historical-type writings in

---

[1] An excellent treatment is Michael Kraus, *The Writing of American History* (Norman: University of Oklahoma Press, 1953). See also William T. Hutchinson (ed.), *The Marcus W. Jernegan Essays in American Historiography* (Chicago: The University of Chicago Press, 1937); Hugh H. Bellot, *American History and American Historians* (London: The Athlone Press, 1952); Harvey Wish, *The American Historian: A Social-Intellectual History of the Writing of the American Past* (New York: Oxford University Press, 1960); George P. Gooch, *History and Historians in the 19th Century* (2nd ed.; London: Longmans, Green, 1913—Reprinted New York: Peter Smith, 1949); John S. Bassett, *The Middle Group of American Historians* (New York: The Macmillan Company, 1917); and most recently, John Higham, Leonard Krieger, and Felix Gilbert, *History* (Englewood Cliffs, New Jersey: Prentice-Hall, Inc., 1965).

[2] Special student subscription rates are available. Consult your instructor.

America reflected the prevailing English writing style carried over by the early settlers, i.e., they took the form of the literary essay. The American people had no history, in the modern form of writing it. John Smith's *A True Relation,* an account of the first year in Jamestown and written in 1608, is a case in point. And other colonial figures, such as William Bradford and John Winthrop, wrote similar colonial histories. Thus, for approximately the first one hundred fifty years of her experience, America had no real historical writing.

Nevertheless, throughout the colonial period a number of individuals kept diaries, wrote their memoirs, and composed local "histories," but these were either sporadic or provincial works, or both. They could hardly be termed historical writing.[3] The Revolutionary War, fortunately, provided the first significant spark of a national consciousness in the American people. Leading public figures such as Noah Webster and Benjamin Rush encouraged the people to write American history. In 1783, as a direct result of such efforts, the *Boston Magazine,* a journal devoted to the writing of the history of the Revolutionary War, made its appearance.

With this as a notable beginning, various other historical magazines also made their appearance throughout the 1780's forward. And some local historical societies were formed to perform the invaluable function of preserving and researching local history. The American nation produced some rather good, albeit provincial, state histories during the Revolutionary period. By way of example, Thomas Hutchinson wrote *A History of the Colony of Massachusetts Bay* shortly after the termination of the French and Indian War. Robert Proud wrote a *History of Pennsylvania* during the course of the Revolutionary War and published it afterwards. And Alex Hewat wrote a *History of South Carolina and Georgia* during the same period.

An individual named Parson Weems was also writing a great deal of material, which he very courageously and very optimistically referred to as history. But such was hardly the case. Weems was definitely not an historian: He was a propagandist for Americana, or better still he was an historical moralist in the temper of medieval historians. Not unlike a great many writers at a comparable stage in European historiography, Weems made an effort to romanticize—to sell to the American people—the idea of the American revolution and the new American nation. Weems both hero-worshipped to the point of idolatry and deliberately fabricated stories concerning the founders of the American republic. By way of illustration, he is responsible for the famous George Washington cherry tree story, which has, inciden-

[3] See Kraus, *op. cit.,* Chapter II, for a very thorough account of American history writing in its formative stage.

tally, absolutely no basis in historical fact. Historians are still fighting the widespread popular acceptance of the fiction of Weems and others like him. Still, Parson Weems was well read, and he did perform the notable function of helping to awaken a national consciousness in the American people.

At one point in American history an argument could be developed for the need of this type of material to awaken a national consciousness in the people. Of course, such a technique risks the danger of the pitfall of an intense militaristic nationalism. Be that as it may, when a national grouping does not possess its own heritage, it is forced to create one for its self-preservation. But this does not result in legitimate history writing. Today, however, the United States claims both a real history and a distinct national consciousness. It can solidly claim its fair share of legitimate heroes and bask in their exploits. It also possesses a constantly growing national heritage. Fabrication of historical fact no longer serves any purpose; it has no place in historical writing now nor did it during the days of Parson Weems.

Fortunately, at the very time when Weems was writing his brand of "history," an American national consciousness was emerging. Whether or not his fictitious stories of American greatness contributed toward this development is begging the point. The fact is that it happened. Along with this development there occurred another that was equally necessary for the formulation of a distinctively American school of historiography.

Before the actual writing of history can take place, research must be undertaken. Through patient, time-consuming research, primary source materials must be sought and found. This is both a very difficult and a lengthy process, with little in the way of tangible reward. The career researcher is above all a person of dedication (but by sheer accident he is sometimes rewarded financially—the exception to the rule). It is the good fortune of the American historical profession that during the first few decades of the nineteenth century a handful of such dedicated scholars began collecting and publishing historical documents. Examples of this must include the Niles Collection (1822) on Revolutionary War materials, the Elliot Collection (1827–1830), which consists of five volumes of material on the constitutional debates, and above all, the Peter Force Collection, which consists of nine volumes of materials on the Revolutionary era, collected during the 1830's and the 1840's. Force's collection eventually became known as the American Archives.

The first really national history of the United States to be written by an American was a two-volume work by Timothy Pitkin in 1828, entitled *A Political and Civil History of the United States of America.*

The work was rather weak when compared to modern surveys, but it did provide a beginning. Pitkin's real merit lies in the fact that he repudiated the prevailing provincialism and adopted a national outlook.

The first really significant attempt by a European historian writing about the United States was a four-volume history by the Italian, Carlo Botta, entitled *A History of the War of Independence of the United States of America* (long titles were then in vogue), written in 1809. The fact that a European and not an American had written the first substantial history of the United States helped bring about an American interest in history writing. However, both of the works of Pitkin and Botta were of no lasting value, other than that they were pioneer works. Perhaps a more scholarly history of America was written by the German, Ebeling. Unfortunately, his seven-volume history, written during the first two decades of the nineteenth century, was composed in his native language, and as a result it was known only to very few Americans.

2. THE ROMANTIC SCHOOL OF AMERICAN HISTORIOGRAPHY

Nevertheless, the groundwork had been established for the development of the first truly distinguishable school of American historical writing. Known as the Romantic School, it predominated roughly from 1825 to 1880. Romantic history writing is characterized by general, voluminous works that were strictly narrative in form. They were not very factual or reliable, and these deficiencies were magnified by a near total absence of documented source materials. Concerned primarily with the chronicling of political events, romantic histories purposely idolized and romanticized American events and figures. If acts of stupendous courage were not known, and one had not been mentioned for several pages, one would be fabricated. Great stress was placed on individual feats of greatness, and American historians became as deeply entrenched in the "Great Man" approach as did their English contemporaries. Romantic histories also paid little heed to social and intellectual movements. Noted for their complete absence of objectivity and tolerance (in the pattern of twentieth-century nationalistic propaganda), they represented a very poor form of history writing.

Still, some good has been known to come from evil, and accordingly, some good came from the romantic historians. For instance, during roughly the first half of the romantic period, the name of Jared Sparks deserves mention. Sparks collected and published many volumes of Revolutionary era documents, notably the Washington papers, the Franklin papers, and volumes on revolutionary diplomatic correspondence. The number of volumes in this respect totals close to seventy.

But Sparks was a typical romantic historian. If he happened to discover a document that did not portray the American nation or one of its "heroes" in the most favorable light possible, he would not include it in his published collection. Hence, his work was both biased and loaded with errors; he did not utilize good historical methodology. Despite these shortcomings, however, the efforts of Jared Sparks resulted in a tremendous contribution to American documentary collections. And fortunately, later, more objective historians who made use of these documents were able to uncover and correct most of his errors.

The leader of the Romantic School of American historians, and the reputed father of American history writing, is the Transcendentalist, George Bancroft. He wrote a voluminous history of the United States, with the discovery of the American continent as his starting point. Planning to survey the entire period of American history, Bancroft became bogged down in his beloved Revolutionary period and never completed his projected task. He did, however, add two more volumes during the 1880's, but he was still considerably short of his anticipated objective. It might also be added that he was considerably out of date by this time.

Bancroft's writings contain a curious mixture of good historical method, the prevailing hero worship, a zealous advocacy of both providence and progress views of history, and the thesis that the American nation is divinely inspired to lead the world to a democratic utopia under American dominance. The preface to his work very aptly stated his theme, and it is interesting reading for any student in an American history class. In spite of its obvious drawbacks, when Bancroft's first volume appeared in 1834 it was hailed as the beginning of a distinctively American school of historical writing, and American history writing became fairly well established.

A notable exception to the Romantic School of history writing during its period of dominance was Richard Hildreth. Making the first really significant attempt to avoid the prevailing hero worship theme, Hildreth succeeded quite well. Unfortunately, Hildreth was still guilty of being nonobjective. His writing was most definitely pro-Federalist, but it was nonetheless far superior to the other writings during the period. His six-volume history was written during the years 1849–1851 and carried the story of America from the settling of the continent up through the Compromise of 1821.

Nothing worthwhile of a direct nature was ever accomplished by the Romantic School of American historians. Of an indirect nature, perhaps, they instilled the American people with an intense patriotism for their nation—a patriotism that did not exist in any large measure before the romantics picked up their pens. Although beneficial to the growth of America, this patriotic achievement on the part of the Romantic School historians is not the function of legitimate history. But while writing their highly propagandized version of the past, the romantics were, in the process, creating the proper climate for the establishment of modern historical objectivity. By generating an interest in history they nurtured the development of an historical sense that would eventually destroy the romanticized history they were authoring.

A transitional figure, one who pointed the way toward a brewing change in historical writing, was Francis Parkman. His many volumes were published between 1851–1892. Following the literary rather than the historical narrative style, Parkman nonetheless wrote some classic American history in a most interesting and refreshing manner. He succeeded at times in making accurately portrayed history read like a novel. The profession of history could use many more such stylists as Francis Parkman, provided, of course, that they maintained historical accuracy.

3. THE SCIENTIFIC SCHOOL OF AMERICAN HISTORIOGRAPHY

History writing, in the modern sense, was finally established around 1880 with the development of the Scientific School of American historians. To a large extent based on the style, methodology, and philosophy of the great German scientific historian, Leopold von Ranke, the Scientific School of history writing provides the basis for the modern day historical techniques referred to throughout the work you are reading.

Led by such notables as Andrew White, Daniel Gilman, and Henry Adams, the American Scientific School of historical writing and inquiry possesses many worthwhile and distinguishing characteristics. First, it demands accuracy in quotations, and this results in the quoting of exact statements. Second, it insists on accurate documentation and a copious quantity of footnotes. Third, the Scientific School gives political history its just consideration, but it also takes into account social, cultural, and economic history as well, embracing a much broader perspective than does the preceding Romantic School. Fourth, Scientific School historians, at least during the pioneer stages of the movement, completely ignored previous authors—and quite wisely, we might add. In an attempt to insure historical accuracy they returned to the original sources for their information. Fifth, the Scientific School is also characterized by a considerable amount of debunking—this tendency was also extremely popular during the 1920's. Thus, scientific historians exhibit a temporary tendency to be cynical, and the old heroes of the romantic period, if their heroism had no basis in historical fact, begin to topple one by one. A principal achievement for an early scientifically oriented historian was to solidly establish himself in the profession by destroying some false heroic image.

And finally, the scientific historian, as the name implies, regards history as something of a science, in that facts must be reasonably proven, not assumed. Great stress is placed on the methodology of historical research and writing. As a consequence, the scientific-minded historian soon becomes quite concerned with the proper training of future historians. Expending considerable efforts on this concern, the Scientific School is responsible for history becoming a respectable graduate school endeavor, and the study of history achieves full-time professional status. For along with Von Ranke came the German educational structure, and the Scientific School advocates adopted Von Ranke's seminar technique, the German graduate research degree system, and the detailed graduate study of history in the American educational system.[4] All of these developments were just a part of the German-influenced educational revolution that took place in the United States during the 1880's.

In an effort to further "professionalize" their new disciplinary status, the Scientific School historians organized professional societies and began publishing professional journals. For example, the American Historical Association was founded in 1884, and it inaugurated the *American Historical Review* in 1895. The Mississippi Valley Historical Association was founded in 1907 and shortly afterwards began the publication of the *Mississippi Valley Historical Review*. Originally a regional organization, it gradually broadened in scope, and within a few decades it became a national organization in every way except in name. In 1965, in recognition of this long-standing development, the Mississippi Valley Historical Association officially changed its name to the Society of American Historians and the name of its publication to *The Journal of American History*.

These were notable developments, but there was a more important one. Above all else, the scientific historian made every possible attempt to be objective in the interpretation of his historical fact. Within the rather restrictive limits of human nature he succeeded quite well in this respect. This characteristic is without a doubt the scientific historian's most noteworthy contribution to the discipline of

---

[4] Bear these characteristics of critical or scientific history in mind when we discuss European historiography in the next chapter.

history. Outstanding examples of scientific-minded historians who were pioneers in the objective orientation must include the names of Edward Channing and Henry Adams.

With the advent of the Scientific School and its various characteristics, the American historian began to specialize in a particular area or period. This development quickly gave rise to a number of schools of interpretation and emphasis within the framework of the new scientific method.

Nationalist School   Historically, the first such Scientific School of specialization to arise was the Nationalist School of historical interpretation. The nationalistic historians upheld as their key tenet the idea that the development of a strong nation-state should be the major objective of any people. Hence, they displayed a marked tendency to deify the nation. Writing primarily during the Age of Big Business, the nationalists equated national progress with individual material prosperity. They had a very high regard for property rights, and consequently they adopted a rather conservative approach to change.

A list of noted nationalistic historians would include: John B. McMaster, who introduced studies of the "common man" in his volumes and thereby paved the way for the eventual development of American social history; and James Rhodes, John Burgess, and John Fiske, who upheld the "white man's burden" theory. Incidentally, when McMaster began his studies of the common man, the so-called Great Man approach to the study of history began to decline.

Internationalist School   Arising in part to counteract the nationalists and in part to achieve an even greater degree of objectivity (the nationalists were avowedly partisan) were the internationalists, also known as the imperialists—a term subject to misinterpretation. Adherents of this school refused to regard the United States as being strictly "American" and stressed the fact that America was at one time British. Like the nationalists, the internationalists also favored their own nation, but being more objective, they were willing to acknowledge the tremendous influences that Great Britain in particular and Europe in general rendered to the development of the United States. These historians possessed a much wider perspective than did their nationalistic contemporaries. As a consequence, they were able to write their histories of the colonial period in a much more objective manner. Notable examples of internationalist-type historians were George Beer, Herbert Osgood, and Lawrence Gipson.

Sectionalist School   While nationalists and internationalists were conducting a battle over the origins and nature of the American nation, a third fragment of the Scientific School silently developed, crept into the historical arena, and permanently remained there. In the absence of a better term, we might allude to this third group as the sectionalists. Highly conscious of the complexities of American life and culture, the sectionalists believed that by thoroughly investigating the history of a particular region they could gain further insight in and understanding of the American nation as a whole. The sectionalist school was originally a western school, for this section of the country—the frontier—was obviously and traditionally the most "national" type section of the nation in character. Therefore, its character undoubtedly exerted great influence on the national character—at least, this was the primary assumption of this school.

This western sectionalistic school, better known as the Frontier School, exhibited some very prominent American historians on its membership rolls. Hubert H. Bancroft, for instance, wrote some twenty-eight volumes on the Far West and collected tens of thousands of documents. Reuben G. Thwaites wrote well over one hundred volumes, primarily on western travel and Jesuit missionary activity. Herbert E. Bolton concentrated on the Spanish borderlands—that geographical area where Anglo, Latin, and Indian cultures met and clashed. This subject, incidentally, is a very rich field for investigation.

But by far the biggest name among these giant-sized western sectional historians was that of Frederick Jackson Turner. According to the "Turner thesis," the frontier experience, coupled with American expansion into an area of free land, molded the character and institutions of modern day America. The Turnerite interpretation is gradually losing its influence; a modern but moderate exponent is the well-known historian, Ray Allen Billington.

Prompted by the successes of the westerners, other historians began to concentrate on other portions of the country. For example, Ulrich B. Phillips and William E. Dodd wrote extensively on southern contributions to the American nation. Samuel E. Morison and James T. Adams did likewise for New England.

The Cultural School   At the very time when the sectionalists were making their big push, a fourth fragmentation of the Scientific School was in the making. For lack of a better term, and fully admitting to its probable deficiencies, let us refer to this school as the Cultural School. The word "cultural" will be used in its broadest possible sense. It is very difficult to give this school an adequate label. Some historians refer to it as the "New History," but the movement is broader than a sociological-integrated approach to interpretation that the New History advocates. The group of historians who belong to the Cultural

School emphasizes various areas of human behavior and the effect of this behavior on the development of American society.

The Cultural School was given major impetus by Dixon Ryan Fox and Arthur M. Schlesinger with their thirteen-volume *A History of American Life*, begun in 1928, which was an attempt to integrate and correlate the various social sciences in an effort to better understand and interpret the human past. Cultural historians choose specific topics of personal interest, e.g., literature, economics, folklore, philosophy, sociology, etc., and then write the histories of these subjects and indicate their influence on the development of American ideas, attitudes, and practices.

One extremely influential historian who fits into this grouping is Charles Beard. In his "Economic Interpretations" of the formation of the Constitution and of the Jeffersonian era, Beard's view was that economic factors have shaped American institutions, government, and subsequent developments. He would synthesize historical fact and economic principles in an effort to explain the past. Beard was careful to point out, however, that economic motives alone did not explain America, just as Turner would indicate that more than the frontier experience was required to create the American character.

The advocates of both men, the "Beardians" and the "Turnerians," were and oftentimes are too zealous. The disciples quite often push the thesis of their masters further than was originally intended, causing some very interesting and colorful battles between the adherents of the various schools of interpretation. Any historical thesis should be accepted strictly for what it is—a thesis. The formulators of theses are usually more prone to admit probable deficiencies in their theories than are their disciples.

Modern Trends Many historians still belong to either the Turner or the Beard school. And it goes without saying that the theses of both historians, while having some adherents, have been attacked and criticized from many quarters. But there is a growing number of historians who, in the tradition of Fox and Schlesinger, pursue the integrated cultural aspect of the American experience. Partially triggered by James Harvey Robinson's lectures on European intellectual history at Columbia and his subsequent development of the "New History," these historians include Vernon Parrington, Ralph Gabriel, and Merle Curti. Such historians emphasize the role and importance of ideas, culture, and social institutions in attempting to explain the United States.

This "intellectual" approach to the study of history, which is a movement within the Cultural School, has resulted in a number of notable developments on the contemporary scene. Several programs in

American Studies, emphasizing an integration of history with literature, philosophy, and other related disciplines, have been initiated. The Ph.D. degree, which traditionally has reflected training in research techniques and scholarship, is also the standard, academic credential for university teaching and is being conferred, for example, in the "History of Ideas" and the "History of Science."

The intellectual approach is an extremely difficult one in that it presupposes not only a thorough grounding in history but a rather detailed mastery of one or more other related disciplines as well. It is a thoroughly integrated approach to the past of mankind. Of course, it cannot be stressed too much that man is an extremely complex creature. There is no easy way to explain his actions.

A pioneer in the intellectual area is Dixon Ryan Fox, whose *Ideas in Motion* provides major impetus for the movement. *The Growth of American Thought,* authored by Merle Curti, is a monumental, contemporary, Pulitzer-Prize-winning study on the subject. Other historians—Richard Hofstadter and Clinton Rossiter are cases in point—attempt to explain American political behavior in terms of the growth and development of particular ideologies. Theirs is an intellectual approach to political history. Other prominent members of the school include William Cash, Perry Miller, and Loren Baritz. The area of intellectual history is fertile ground for new and refreshing studies on the American nation.

We have already seen how various historians have attempted to discover the basic factors of human behavior by discovering "laws" and by emphasizing economic factors, geographical factors, etc. Throughout the twentieth century there has been a growing tendency to interpret past human behavior in terms of the disciplines of human behavior, *viz.,* sociology and psychology, particularly the former.

The sociological approach to historical interpretation is reflective of Robinson's "New History," even though Robinson himself emphasized the need for the wide integration of factors in historical study rather than a detailed application of sociological principles alone. The key to the approach is an emphasis on the role of environment in shaping human actions. Hence, a knowledge of social evolution and the principles of social organization must become part of the working tools of the professional historian. Max Weber and Karl Lamprecht are early examples of German scholars who employed this technique.

As we move further into the twentieth century, the trend begins to concentrate on a slightly different factor: motivation. An analysis of the motivation of the characters on the historical stage has become extremely important in formulating an intelligent appraisal of the human past. With this development there appears an increasing concern for the utilization of the scientific apparatus of sociology, and for the methodology and theorizing of psychology.

Real impetus for the new techniques (which find their origins in the World War II era) results from a series of lectures given by the historian, David M. Potter, at the University of Chicago in 1950. These lectures emphasized the contributions of the behavioral scientist to an interpretation of the American character and pleaded for the utilization of behavioral techniques in historical inquiry. The ideas which Potter put forth find practical application in his *People of Plenty*.

Building upon the base established by Potter is C. G. Hempel. He introduced the use of a model of social systems against which suspected historical laws or patterns would be tested. J. S. Bruner adds the use of concept analysis to the working tools of the "behavioral historian." [5]

The behavioral approach as it is applied to political science, i.e., the statistical approach that employs the theory of games, bloc behavior patterns, and other devices, does not find direct application to most aspects of history. The discipline is not so constructed. However, the behavioral findings of the political scientists can and do add to the reservoir of fact utilized by the historian in his interpretations.

Unfortunately, a work occasionally appears that attempts to apply the techniques of psychology to an historical figure, as if that figure were currently pouring out his soul to a skilled psychiatrist. When working with a live subject the psychiatrist is often unable to pinpoint difficulties. The problem is compounded tremendously when one tries to analyze someone who has been dead for decades or centuries. This approach does not constitute good historical inquiry, nor is it a legitimate behavioral approach. [6]

The proper application of the behavioral technique is quite difficult. Some historians will not accept it, claiming that it destroys history as a distinct discipline and makes it subsidiary to sociology or some other "social science." Consequently, the "behavioral" historian must exercise great care in making a distinction between description and explanation in his use of such tools. He properly uses them to explain the behavior of his characters; the sociologist, for example, utilizes a descriptive technique. He is interested in institutions as they

[5] For a thorough treatment of recent behavioral trends see N. L. Gage (ed.), *Handbook of Research on Teaching* (Chicago: Rand McNally and Company, 1963).

[6] One of the most recent of these works, which has been widely criticized by historians in published reviews, is Sigmund Freud and William C. Bulleit, *Thomas Woodrow Wilson: Twenty-Eighth President of the United States, A Psychological Study* (Boston: Houghton Mifflin Company, 1967).

evolve into the present scheme of things, whereas the historian is concerned with these same institutions only as they affect his characters and provide adequate explanations for past behavior.

If the statement made at the beginning of this work—which was to the effect that the broader the perspective of the individual historian, the greater should be his degree of attained objectivity—has any validity, current trends in American historical research should prove highly fruitful in the very near future.

EUROPEAN HISTORIOGRAPHY

6

European historiography constitutes an extremely complex study, especially when compared with American historiography, owing to the vast time period involved—some 2500 years. Obviously, then, some sweeping generalizations will have to be made in order to survey this material in a single chapter, for entire books have been written on particular phases of European historiography.

Another reason for the complexity of European historiography is the vast number of countries involved. It cannot be hoped to detail here the development of historiography for all of the nations that appeared and disappeared during the course of European history. Hence, an arbitrary decision must be made: This chapter will concentrate primarily on the historiography of the major countries of Europe and only mention the other countries whenever generalized observations are possible. Bear in mind that the purpose of this work is to serve simply as an introduction, not as a definitive study.[1]

---

[1] For detailed reading see James W. Thompson and Bernard J. Holm, *A History of Historical Writings* (2 vols.; New York: The Macmillan Company, 1942); Bernadotte E. Schmitt, *Some Historians of Modern Europe* (Chicago: The University of Chicago Press, 1942); George P. Gooch, *History and Historians in the 19th Century* (New York: Longmans, Green, 1948); James T. Shotwell, *The History of History*, Vol. I (New York: Columbia University Press, 1939); Harry E. Barnes, *A History of Historical Writing* (2nd rev. ed.; New York: Dover Publications, Inc., 1963); Matthew A. Fitzsimons, Alfred G. Pundt, and Charles E. Nowell (eds.), *The Development of Historiography* (Harrisburg, Pennsylvania: The Stackpole Company, 1954); and S. William Halperin, *Some Twentieth-Century Historians* (New York: Alfred A. Knopf, Inc., 1961).

1. GRECO-ROMAN HISTORY WRITING

Probably the pioneer historian in the Western world was Homer, but by modern standards we could hardly consider the epic themes of the *Iliad* and the *Odyssey* to be good history.[2] Homer did give us some of the history of his age, and subsequent writers transformed the Homerian epic into the narrative form—the style used today. But in terms of objectivity and tolerance, these early Greek writers were unable to divorce themselves from their gods, and consequently much of their history is legend and myth. They are important for no other reason than the fact that they provided an acceptable writing form for historical inquiry.

Upon this base Herodotus wrote his famous *History of the Persian Wars*. He viewed these wars as a clash between two different cultures and felt it necessary to delve into an explanation of these cultures. Attempting to be objective, he gave due credit to the hated Persians for their accomplishments. Because of this, and despite the weaknesses in Greek historical interpretation brought on by the widespread acceptance of gods, myth, and legend in their historical writings, Herodotus has been commonly regarded as the "father of history."

Building upon Herodotus was Thucydides, who wrote a history of the Peloponnesian War. Thucydides was the first true historian in that he sought to assess causes, insisted upon accuracy, and attained a fair degree of objectivity. Of equal importance was his insistence on the utility of historical study for coping with future, similar problems. His major weakness was an overemphasis on political matters, and as a result, Thucydides unknowingly established a pattern that remained quite strong until the nineteenth century, *viz.*, the dominating concern for political issues in historical writing.

Perhaps this development, which was due to the insistence of Thucydides on utility, also caused Greek history writing to lose much of its flavor over the next few centuries. The writings of later historians were undertaken primarily to instruct the reader in moral principles. Hence, historical technique was allowed to suffer. But Polybius restored the tradition of Herodotus and Thucydides in his history of the Punic Wars era, and again, accuracy, objectivity, and utility were being emphasized jointly.

Early Roman history was strongly influenced by the preceding Greek history. This is borne out by the fact that the first Roman historian, Pictor (ca. 250 B.C.), wrote his account of the Punic Wars

---

[2] The authenticity of much of Homer's *Odyssey*, however, is interestingly presented in Ernle Bradford, *Ulysses Found* (New York: Harcourt, Brace & World, 1963).

in the Greek language. The first Roman historian to write in Latin was Cato, a half-century later.

A major popularizer of Roman history writing was Julius Caesar. His *Commentaries on the Gallic Wars* and his later *Commentaries on the Civil War* emphasized objectivity, clarity, and a high degree of accuracy, even though Caesar wrote primarily to establish his own reputation. A contemporary writer, Sallust, was important in that he attempted to assess the character and the values of the aristocracy. Thus his work tended toward the moralistic—but Polybius had long before stated that the historian must make value judgments.

One of the really big names in any consideration of Roman historiography was that of Livy. Unfortunately, Livy was not greatly concerned with accuracy and objectivity. He wrote with the obvious intent of selling Rome to the Romans (a Roman equivalent to Parson Weems?). But Livy did succeed in giving the modern historian a rather clear insight into the spirit and times of the early Romans.

The next and last great figure in Roman historiography was Tacitus, who died around 120 A.D. Employing some of the scientific techniques exemplified by Polybius, Tacitus in his famous *Annals* and *Histories* attempted to give an impartial account of the decline of Roman greatness. Yet his personal prejudices were obvious. His real strength was his ability to analyze the political intrigue that characterized his age. In another work, more sociological than historical, *Germania*, Tacitus gave the world its best account of the Teutonic movement into imperial Rome.

Some generalizations on Greco-Roman historiography can now be attempted. There was some progress being made in the development of historical writing and technique. Most historians at least tried to be accurate and objective in their work. The main deficiency of the historians of the ancient world was due simply to the fact that they were under the influence of their own cultural milieu. The influence of the gods, myth, and undocumented legend continually crept into their writings. Nonetheless, the crude essentials for the rigorous writing of history were established. These would be perfected in time.

2. EARLY CHRISTIAN HISTORICAL WRITING

Christianity brought an abrupt change to the tenor of historical writing; unfortunately, it was a retrogressive change. The works of the Greek and Roman historians were largely spurned. After all, they were the products of pagan minds. This closed-minded attitude naturally resulted in another detrimental effect on history. Early Christian writers were openly and avowedly not objective. Not only were they hostile to any achievement by a pagan culture, but their interpretations were slanted in such a manner so as to make Christianity appear as favorable as possible, even to the point of bending or overlooking facts in order to do so. In this respect, early Christian writers, e.g., Eusebius and Jerome, offered nothing of importance to historical writing.

However, early Christian authors did make contributions to the discipline of history in other respects. Augustine's *City of God,* unlike the works of the pagans, proposed an end (teleological view) for history, whereas the pagans had been content with a cyclical interpretation. Thus, Christian historians formulated the first real philosophy of history.[3] Early Christians also sought to establish a longstanding heritage for their beliefs in an effort to attract converts to their religion. This they were able to do through the use of the Old Testament as an historical document. But in order to indicate a continuity between Hebrew and Christian thought, they found it necessary to develop chronologies of the past. Thus, it came about that the *Chronicles* of Jerome, a translation and amplification of an earlier work by Eusebius, became the basis for chronological reckoning in the Western world, and it was destined to be a system that would last well into modern times.

With the fall of Roman civilization in the west in 476 A.D., the first distinguishable school of European historiography made its appearance. The medieval period had begun, and Europe, as we commonly regard it, was beginning to evolve.

3. EARLY MEDIEVAL HISTORIOGRAPHY

Medieval historiography may be introduced with some broad statements. Generally speaking, medieval historians combined theology and historical fact to produce their widespread interpretation of a providentially inspired course of human events. Material developments were given very little attention. This was to be expected in view of the fact that most medieval historians were Christian monks. These men tended to reshape historical fact, if deemed necessary, in order to present their religious beliefs in the best possible light. This does not mean to imply that these writers deliberately deceived their readers. So sincerely and thoroughly were they convinced of the validity of their beliefs that in most instances they were unable even to approach objectivity.

Cause-and-effect relationships were also in sorry shape in the hands of the early medievalists. An intervening providence was the easiest

---

[3] The reader is referred to the sections on cyclical and providential philosophies of history in Chapter 3.

and most generally used explanation for any given historical happening. And the works of the pagan historians, regardless of their factual merits, received very little perusal, except perhaps to illustrate the presence of the forces of evil in the world.

An important representative figure of the early medieval period is Gregory of Tours, the author of *History of the Franks*. As a history, Gregory's work leaves much to be desired, but it does provide us with our only detailed account of the Merovingian Period. Gregory, as well as other churchmen-authors of the period, emphasized the role of the Church in its society. His work contains numerous allusions to miracles, not to mention a sermonic quality. But what made Gregory popular was the fact that he wrote in vernacular Latin, a writing form more readily understood by a larger number of people. Venerable Bede, the author of *Ecclesiastical History of the English People,* wrote in the same temper, but Bede tended to play down the role of miracles in history and attempted to be more judicious in choosing his source materials.

Moving into the ninth century—the period of the Carolingian Renaissance—the writing of history began an upward sweep. And any consideration of European historiography must begin to take into account the existence of various national groupings. Charlemagne commenced a revival of letters, and history, including a consideration for the pagan historians of the ancient world, became a part of the Carolingian educational structure.

Charlemagne required the various monasteries in his realm to keep accurate records. Consequently, monks made rather cryptic notations on what of importance happened during a particular season or year. These "annals" as they were called, consisted of nothing more than straightforward report accounts; they rarely contained any interpretation or comment. One could not ask for greater objectivity or for a more valuable source of factual information about the medieval period, although much was left to be desired in terms of an interesting writing style.

In most instances these annals were combined, expanded with some additional fact or a bit of interpretation, and called chronicles. In many cases a chronicle was a very provincial work. It would cover the "history" of a particular monastery or town. But over a period of approximately two centuries, these chronicles began to develop into something approaching historical writing. The *Chronicle* of Otto of Freising (see below) in the twelfth century was indicative of this new tendency. The development of annals and chronicles comprised the outstanding events of early medieval historiography.

Beginning with the eleventh century, considerable change was taking place. Europe, reintroduced to the ancient Near East through the Crusades and to a new "pagan" group, the Vikings, was beginning to pay a little more attention to secular matters. Also instrumental in effecting this change in attitude was the growing number of political difficulties in a splintering Europe, which was resulting in the crude beginnings of nations. As a consequence, even though churchmen were still responsible for most historical writing, outside pressures were forcing them to give considerably more attention to secular matters than they had been giving formerly.

There were no full-time historians during the Middle Ages, and history was not offered as a distinct discipline in the rising university. History remained, as in the Carolingian period, a part of the subject matter of grammar. No individuals attempted to standardize the writing format or the methodology of history. No real attempt was made to delve into the past, for most historians were primarily concerned with their own times. They were content with providing some sort of a record of their own age, along with some general instructions on morality.

Otto of Freising characterizes medieval historiographic study. Although careless in the handling of details, he did make use of reliable sources, and his work is considered important by modern medievalists. Yet since Otto was a bishop, he was biased against secular affairs and thereby presented a moralistic slant to his interpretations. Nonetheless, Otto did make an attempt to consider causes and effects. Unfortunately, his religious office partially blinded him from an objective analysis of the secular world.

Moving into the later Middle Ages, increasing attention was being given to record keeping and document collecting. Many feudal lords began employing clerks, and as a result more detailed chronicles were being compiled. As time passed, these became broader in scope and provided the future historian worthwhile tools with which to reconstruct the past.

4. RENAISSANCE HISTORIOGRAPHY

The period of the Renaissance was an era of renewed interest in antiquity, the classics, and literary criticism. It was an age when the study of man became important; it was an age of secularization. Consequently, the Renaissance era produced some notable developments in the field of historiography.

The interest in antiquity resulted in the writing of history from a less provincial viewpoint. No longer were historians simply the chroniclers of their own times; the past began to find a place in historical writing and inquiry. Pagan histories were being studied and imitated.

The result was greater concern for secular activities. Writers became more critical of their own works and the works of others. The convenient utilization of an intervening providence to explain human affairs was giving way somewhat to a determination of proximate and remote causation. Above all, the true humanistic historian desired truth.

But truth was not always present. History was still not a full-time profession. Writers required patrons in order to support their work. Quite naturally, the historical works of these writers oftentimes made the patron, whether individual or institution, a little more likeable than the facts would warrant. Thus, history writing had not yet arrived at the time when proper emphasis was placed on historical objectivity.

Nonetheless, interest in historical studies was improving tremendously. Interest in the classics resulted in the feverish search for the lost manuscripts of antiquity, and some individuals collected and published documents and sources. Publishing, incidentally, was aided considerably by the invention of the printing press, a decided boon for the destruction of the old provincialism, which was being replaced by an emphasis on nationalism.

The father of Renaissance history writing, or humanism as the literary style was termed, was Francesco Petrarch (1304–1374). Petrarch wrote on the civilizations of the ancient classical era and succeeded in debunking some of the myths dealing with the Roman period. Although he did not utilize good historical method, he did champion interest in historical study. And this interest was no better witnessed than in Florence, one area in the Italies with a civilization conducive to the development of historical works. Hence, near the end of the Italian Renaissance, Machiavelli (1469–1527) performed real yeoman service in determining causes for historical events. Machiavelli marked the change-over from a providential to a definite, secular orientation in history. He also stressed the need for historical study in explaining political affairs, thus giving history a definite, practical application.

Beyond the Italies the influence of the Renaissance was felt a little later. Of particular importance was Jean Bodin, a Frenchman who wrote the first major work on historical method. In this work, *Method for Easily Understanding History*, Bodin emphasized the need for proper interpretation of source materials and placed major stress on geographical factors in shaping human events.

While the Renaissance was bringing about the aforementioned changes in historiography, the Reformation rocked the unity of medieval Christendom. Historical writing, except for the concurrent humanistic movement, became involved in the religious controversies of the day. For a time history again dwelt on theology; it was characterized by a moralistic spirit quite similar to that of the early Middle Ages.

5. REFORMATION HISTORIOGRAPHY

The writing of history became the writing of propaganda during the Reformation era. Objectivity was temporarily forgotten. History became purely utilitarian; its purpose was to sway converts to either the Catholic or the Protestant point of view. A good result of this, however, was the penetrating search for historical documents, even though the motivation of the document seekers was far from commendable. Catholics sought to prove beyond any doubt, on the basis of historical fact, that Protestantism was the anti-Christ. And Protestants were equally convinced that Catholics were the agents of the devil. Both camps sought to add respectability and credence to their positions by adequate documentation. As a result, a considerable number of heretofore unknown historical documents were discovered and published.

Among Protestant historians a favorite device was to point out the cruelty of Catholic persecutions. John Foxe, in *The Acts and Monuments of the Christian Martyrs* (1563), definitely portrayed this theme. The *Magdeburg Centuries,* edited by Flacius, monumentally surveyed the story of Christianity with the planned intent of proving that the Church of Rome had deliberately subverted true Christianity. Another prominent historian among the Protestants was Phillip Milanchthon, but more objective was John Knox, one of the few Reformation era polemicists to present the historical facts in a reasonably honest manner. The work of Sleidanus is also worthy of mention, not for his contribution to the Protestant cause, but rather for his indirect contributions to the discipline of history. Sleidanus made ample use of original historical documents and other works to emphasize political factors as causes for the Reformation.

The Catholic counterblast was very ably led by Baronius, whose *Ecclesiastical Annals* outrivals the *Magdeburg Centuries* in sheer venom. Baronius collected a vast number of documents but judiciously used only those which furthered the Catholic cause. Such deception, common among polemicists in both camps, could hardly be termed good history. Another supporter of the Catholic cause, Bossuet, wrote without the passions of his contemporaries. A definite partisan, he nonetheless attempted a degree of objectivity uncommon in his chaotic age. He also presented one of the last pleas for a providential view of historical interpretation. But Bossuet's works do not really constitute good history.

6. RATIONALIST SCHOOL OF HISTORIOGRAPHY

During the time when Europe was embroiled in religious controversy, foreboding changes in other realms were in the making. This was due primarily to Europe's geographical and intellectual expansion. Columbus, Da Gama, Magellan, and Hudson were discovering the size and scope of the world, while individuals such as Richard Hakluyt popularized their findings. Intellectual giants of the caliber of Galileo, Descartes, and Newton were laying the groundwork for a veritable revolution in intellectual thought and attitude.

Descartes had succeeded in wiping out the philosophical authoritarianism of the past; man's mind was now free to doubt anything. And the Newtonian World Machine was indeed a wonderful discovery. There was an order to the universe, which had been unknown since the beginning of time. These laws of nature were within the grasp of human knowledge. Mankind needed only faith in man to achieve tremendous wonders. John Locke suggested a new philosophy based on empirical observation (sense perception), and the Frenchman, Fontenelle, predicted continued progress for humanity.

These developments made possible an intellectual climate ripe for the formation of some really notable advances in historical writing. One of the most worthwhile characteristics of this change in attitude was a marked tendency to broaden the scope of historical study. Known as the Rationalist School of historical writing, it considered the social, cultural, and economic aspects of human endeavor as well as the traditional theological and political aspects of the subject.

In keeping with the prevailing Enlightenment philosophy this school of history writing emphasized the intellect of man as the decisive factor in human developments rather than the old providential notion. Another Enlightenment belief, that environment shapes human behavior, also influenced historical writing. Hence, historians emphasized climate, geography, and social and political institutions in attempting to explain human behavior. There was a definite humanitarian thread running throughout rationalistic works.

The Enlightenment produced new developments in historiography. Rationalist history was marked by attempts to write world or "universal" histories, giving rise to periodization. The Dutchman, Cellarius, divided history into ancient, medieval, and new periods. Although rationalistic historians attempted to be objective, they wrote with a definite end in mind. Historical fact always proves, according to their interpretation, that mankind advances whenever the human race is not being tyrannized. This insistence on a progress view of history was one of the biggest characteristics of the school.

Giambattista Vico (1668–1744) was representative of this belief.

In his writings the old notion of a gradually declining culture is replaced by the continuous development of processes that bring about the steady progress of humanity. And in such a frame of reference, miracles become unnecessary in justifying history. Natural laws are considered far better. Vico devised a spiral-type progress: Society is moving in cycles, but they are upward-moving cycles. Interestingly enough, Vico and his progress-believing contemporaries were taking a conservative approach to progress because they could not anticipate the enormous technological and scientific advances that soon came about. It should be pointed out that the most widely attributed cause for the lack of progress in the past had been the alleged tyrannical nature of authoritarian religion. Hence, most early progress-believers attacked organized religion.

The most prominent of all rationalist historians was Edward Gibbon (1737–1794), whose classic The History of the Decline and Fall of the Roman Empire is still widely read. Gibbon's work is characterized by good style and organization, a very accurate portrayal of facts, and a popular theme. He enjoyed a great reputation among his contemporaries as well as among modern historians. Gibbon believed that historians should be literary artists, not researchers, and he disparaged manuscript work, utilizing only the best printed works he could find. Yet at the same time he encouraged others to engage in manuscript study and codification. In his writing Gibbon emphasized political and martial affairs, playing down social, cultural, and economic aspects—although they did receive mention. In this respect, he exhibited a narrow view of the content of history. Be that as it may, much of his work still stands as the best that has been written on such a monumental scale.

Some rationalist historians tended to stress emotionality rather than rationality, and thus they unknowingly provided a logical bridge to the romanticism of the next historiographic period.

7. ROMANTIC HISTORIOGRAPHY

The Reformation had weakened religious faith, and the ideas of the Enlightenment, as reflected by the French Revolution, were considered by many to have been repudiated. The romantic reaction to Enlightenment rationality was nothing more than an attempt to fill a religious and intellectual vacuum.

Romanticists believed in what is termed the cultural evolution of society, to which was added a solidarity of the human race concept. Emotion and personal feeling were stressed at the expense of the preceding rationality. The era witnessed a pronounced tendency to escape reality—to escape to the peace and beauty of nature, or to escape to far off places or far distant periods in history.

But the Enlightenment idea of natural rights was maintained and pushed to its extreme. Man became totally free; therefore, any artificial restriction placed upon him by society was wrong. The romantic historians demonstrated a high degree of sympathy toward social reform or political liberalism—any cause which might further individual freedom. Romantics were ardent nationalists and aided in the development of national literatures. They were equally ardent in their exposition of the "Great Man" theory [4] of history; after all, individuality received significant stress in their thinking. Running throughout romantic thought was a certain mystical quality. There is an unseen guiding spirit that is directing man in his cultural evolution.

One of the many great romantic school historians was Chateaubriand (1768–1848), a Frenchman who began his historical career rather conservatively. Following a religious conversion, Chateaubriand wrote his classic *Genius of Christianity,* in which he stressed the role of Christianity as the stimulus for the development of art and poetry and for human progress. Chateaubriand was very literary in his style and was very much concerned with presenting detailed accounts of the physical setting of historical events. Pictorial descriptions were emphasized. Like other romantic historians, he had a penchant for hero worship and local color, and, imbued with nationalism and patriotism for his own country, he treated his nation's past with a certain sentimentality. This particular aspect of romantic writing was especially utilized by German romantics.

8. NATIONALIST HISTORIOGRAPHY

Seeds of nationalistic thought were found throughout romantic writings. Further impetus was given by the French Revolution and its influence on inculcating a nationalistic spirit in such countries as Germany and Spain. And no small influence came from the pen of Gobineau, who proclaimed a racist superiority in 1854. German thinkers in particular used his racist idea to support their nationalist school of history writing.

The Englishman, Thomas Macaulay, is representative of the nationalist school. Like other nationalist historians, Macaulay wrote to glorify his nation's past. In this respect his famous work, *History of England,* was partisan, as were all other nationalistic histories. But Macaulay did display good analysis, and he made a brilliant contribution to historical literature, even if he did not make an equal contribution to historical method.

[4] The Great Man theory holds that history is the study of the biographies of the great leaders of given eras. Hence, the names "Age of Philip II," "Age of Louis XIV," and "Napoleonic Europe" are given to various historical periods.

9. CRITICAL-SCIENTIFIC HISTORIOGRAPHY

In roughly the latter half of the nineteenth century, overlapping the romantic and nationalistic schools of historical interpretation, is found what might be regarded as either the critical or scientific school. Many of the adherents of this school may also exhibit some of the characteristics of either romantic or nationalistic writing.

Some progress in the direction of critical history writing had been made by the humanists, but this progress had been largely stifled by the events of the Reformation era. The Maurists, a group of Benedictine monks at Saint Maur in France, had developed the rudiments of critical historiography in the late seventeenth and early eighteenth centuries. The romantic conception of history as a broad evolving process gave further rise to the development of a critical historical method. Also instrumental was the growing nationalistic spirit, which led to a greater concern for proving or disproving, as the case may be, the accuracy of historical facts.

Probably the chief initiator of modern critical historiography was Barthold Niebuhr. His *Roman History* reflected considerable testing of the traditional documents and writings. But the outstanding figure in the school was Leopold von Ranke. He established the methodology for determining the authenticity of source materials, insisted on historical truth, and developed the notion of "inner criticism," i.e., studying the habits and attitudes of the author in order to better evaluate his interpretations. Von Ranke also insisted upon detached, objective assessment of the facts and put forth the idea that every age and every nation is dominated by some particular ideology that explains its behavior.

Francois Guizot (1787–1874) was the French equivalent of Von Ranke. He did considerable compiling and editing of documents on French history, and in this respect he was a nationalist. Guizot also organized the scientific movement in his country and established the French Historical Society as well. His *General History of European Civilization* was one of the first efforts at a European synthesis—Guizot was especially strong at synthesis. In this category Guizot held an advantage over Von Ranke, who was enmeshed in German history; yet in an overall evaluation Von Ranke was probably the better scholar.

10. TWENTIETH-CENTURY EUROPEAN OVERVIEW

Modern historical writing and research in Europe have both gained and lost owing to twentieth-century chaos. Two bloody wars, and the economic dislocation and suffering that were their aftermath, hardly provided a contemplative atmosphere for historical inquiry. Yet these very wars nurtured a growing interest in historical study and caused historians, despite their handicaps, to make a renewed attempt to discover the reasons for their chaotic age.

Twentieth-century historical writing in France has been affected considerably by two major invasions from Germany and their subsequent psychological effect. No doubt this provides some explanation for the fact that some French historians have largely ignored the last hundred years of their history. But there are some French historians who are seeking answers for the twentieth century and have written some penetrating and objective studies of their nation.

Pierre Renouvin is one French historian who deals with the modern era, specializing in diplomatic history. In his capacity as a diplomatic historian, Renouvin has done considerable editing, e.g., *French Diplomatic Documents, 1871–1914*. He has made a concerted effort to be objective about the causes of World War I (a subject about which Frenchmen are normally quite partisan), and he does a good job, although at times an unconscious anti-German attitude seeps through. Renouvin is strong on historical synthesis, and this is especially important for a diplomatic historian. In various later works he has covered diplomatic history through 1945.

The major concern of many modern French historians is the French Revolution. Another major trend is an emphasis on social and economic history, and yet another important development in French historiography is the appearance of the monumental historical series, in which numerous authors write sections on their own special periods and topics. In this respect, Ernest Lavisse is an important individual. Under his direction a nine volume *History of France From its Origins to the Revolution*, a ten volume *History of Contemporary France From the Revolution to the Peace of 1919*, and, his most important, *Peoples and Civilizations* have been written. However, these works have not been translated into English. Other joint projects included *General History* and *Evolution of Humanity*.

In England, too, the modern trend is to the multi-volumed historical series. The *Cambridge Modern History* (13 volumes), the *Cambridge Medieval History* (8 volumes), and the *Cambridge Ancient History* (12 volumes) reflect this trend. Another such work is the *Oxford History of England*.

Prior to World War I, English historians were concerned with studies of the common man and studies on the British imperial and diplomatic systems. The first consideration reflected the reform spirit then prevalent; the second reflected the peculiar nature of the Commonwealth system. The concern for diplomatic studies has continued throughout the twentieth century, with major impetus having been provided by the release of numerous "secret" documents during the inter-war period. English historians are engaged in a continual revision of their past studies and have exhibited a growing interest in economic history.

A representative modern English historian dealing with the contemporary era is Charles Webster. His concern is mainly with the war and diplomacy of the nineteenth and twentieth centuries. And he is quite optimistic about the future fate of mankind. Webster attended the Versailles peace conference at the close of World War I as an English officer and an expert on the Congress of Vienna. As such he gained a detailed, first-hand knowledge of what was transpiring there. During the following decades Webster devoted his energies to prodding various governments to make their diplomatic records available to historians. He was a proponent of the League of Nations and wrote on it. Later on his active role in the formation of the United Nations led to knighthood. Currently, a history of the RAF during World War II is being prepared under the auspices of the English Government. Mention should also be made of Arnold Toynbee.[5] His challenge and response interpretation of history has stimulated many historians to think more meaningfully about the structure and purpose of their discipline.

Revisionism in England has given rise to a quantitative approach to historical interpretation. It is reflected by Sir Lewis Namier, whose *England in the Age of the American Revolution* (1930) utilizes a behavioral approach in attempting to explain why Parliament acted as it did. In effect, Namier and the historians who accept his position attempt to make use of the tools of the behavioral school of political science by directly applying the technique to appropriate aspects of historical inquiry.[6]

A very difficult nation to summarize briefly is modern Germany. The history writing of Germany varies, but a major portion of the twentieth century is characterized by writing that reflects intense nationalism, undemocratic spirit, and control by an elite group. During the world wars, German history writing took the form of propaganda (as in the case with most warring nations). After World War I the primary concern was exoneration of war guilt, and in this task, German historians were aided by the release of many documents by the Weimar government. In the post-World War II era, German historians are attempting to cope with a most difficult situation: the Third Reich and reunification. Yet there is a different theme in modern German historiography. A few writers emphasize human

[5] *Supra,* Chapter 3.
[6] *Supra,* pp. 59–60.

purpose in their philosophy of history. So there is a strand of idealism and optimism running through the historiography of a disillusioned nation. Yet twentieth-century Germany has contributed Friederich Meinecke, who has performed creditable service in strengthening the Von Ranke approach to historical study. Meinecke is widely regarded as the most able historian produced by Germany since Von Ranke. His approach is intellectual, a playing down of institutional and traditional political history and a studying of political ideas to uncover the dominant concepts of each epoch. Considerable attention has been given by Meinecke to the concepts of liberalism and nationalism.

In Russian historiography the major pre-revolutionary emphasis was on economic matters, and this quickly turned into economic determinism. The revolutionary period was dominated by the Marxian philosophy of history. Moving away from the revolution, under Soviet Party direction, emphasis was placed more upon historical fact and less on abstract ideas. But the purpose of contemporary Soviet writers is to instill in the Russian people a sense of nationalism and unity in the Soviet regime.

During World War II the tendency in the Soviet Union was toward wartime propaganda, but this did not affect Russian historiography as much as that of other warring nations, for the simple fact that propaganda had been very much a part of Russian history writing for some time. Politics continue to dominate Russian history today. Those historians who have left Russia have made significant contributions to Russian historiography.

Balkan historiography reflects the changes in Balkan countries in the twentieth century. Up to the end of World War I the dominant trend in writing consisted of an emphasis on independence—hence, nationalistic history. During the inter-war period historians sought to justify independence to the rest of the world by tracing the origins of their respective nations. World War II brought Communist control for the Balkans, and history writing, as in Russia, was used for political purposes.

Among Austrian historians the idea of nationalism was quite strong, first in the treatment of the Dual Monarchy, and then in the "Middle Europe" idea. A more radical nationalism came with Nazi rule. After World War II Austrian historians return to solid scholarship. Austrian medievalists in particular have done a creditable job.

Hungarian historiography is dominated by the independence theme up to World War I; this was at the expense of Austria. During the inter-war period the main theme concerned a penetrating search for the spiritual motivation that was reputed to be at the base of historical fact. Since coming under Communist control, Hungarian historiography has been dominated by political considerations.

In modern Belgian historiography there is an enormous effort to collect archival materials in numerous monographic studies. These are published in the many Belgian professional journals. Belgium's greatest modern historian, Henri Pirenne (d. 1935), is best known for his studies in medieval economic history, but his main concern was with the effect of economic factors on the shaping of society. Imbued in the Von Ranke approach to historical study, Pirenne's interest covered the breadth of Western civilization; he felt the need for synthesis, although he admitted that any synthesizing was necessarily in a constant state of flux. His voluminous writings covered subjects extending well into the 1900's.

Italy has offered little during the twentieth century. The highly influential Benedetto Croce held that history is an art form. Hence history is subject to intuition and the creative impulse—the result, rather nonscientific. World War I brought about a revival of more solid scholarship as Italians sought to discover the reasons for the preceding state of affairs. But fascism from the 1920's forward destroyed objectivity, as is witnessed by the propaganda type of history written. Most good Italian historians today concern themselves with the ancient past.

Spanish history writing reflects an interest in joint projects. History writing was generally liberal for the first three decades of the century and then it broke down under fascist rule. Spanish historians tend to concentrate on the pre-nineteenth century era, particularly on Spain's "Golden Century."

What applies for Spain also applies for Portugal, except for the development pertaining to fascism. Portugal likewise concentrates on her age of greatness. Joint projects are quite popular.

To obtain a detailed knowledge of modern trends in European historiography, one would be forced to consult monographic articles on the subject in the various professional journals. The subject of historiography is exceedingly complex, but no historian is able to function well without a knowledge of it.

One illustration will bear this out. There is currently a historical school known as historical relativism. Adherents believe that the historian accepts as historically true only what his climate of opinion allows him to accept, and that emotional factors create shifts in what is accepted as true from time to time. They further believe that the past is so complex that it can never be known completely, that the only reason for even bothering with it is to obtain some utilitarian value for the present and future. Some historians are guilty of this creation of a changing past, especially those who have held government positions. They occasionally become, in effect, "court historians," and reflect the official government position as it is then being championed. Such views are hardly within the Von Ranke framework of scientific, historical inquiry.

BIBLIOGRAPHY

APPENDIX **A**

A bibliography may have several purposes. One is to inform the reader of those works that the author has consulted in writing his own work. The present bibliography is compiled only partially with this purpose in mind. Most of the information contained in this work is well within the realm of common knowledge for historians, and as a result not many works were formally consulted in writing it. Those works that most influenced the writing of this book are found in the footnotes throughout the book.

A second purpose of a bibliography is to present to the reader an exhaustive list of works written on a particular subject. Again, this is hardly the purpose of the present bibliography. This book is designed to serve as an introductory guide to the discipline of history. It would not be in keeping with this design to list hundreds of advanced texts. Only in the listing of guides to published materials has a degree of thoroughness been attempted. And even here, in consideration of the intended reader, foreign language works and bibliographies, a number of the more obscure and specialized bibliographies, and bibliographies in the area of guides to manuscript materials and collections have been deliberately ignored.

A third purpose of a bibliography is to develop for the benefit of the reader a selected sampling of some of the works available on a given subject for further, more detailed reading. This is the only real claim made for the present bibliography. If the reader should happen to desire a more complete list of works, the bibliographical guides listed in this bibliography, as well as in many of the works themselves, should provide him with whatever information he desires.

For the convenience of the reader the following bibliographical entries are grouped within broad categories of interest.

1. WORKS ON METHODOLOGY

Barzun, Jacques, and Graff, Henry. *The Modern Researcher.* New York: Harcourt, Brace & World, 1957.

83

Becker, Carl. *Everyman His Own Historian.* New York: Appleton-Century-Crofts, 1935.

Bloch, M. *The Historian's Craft.* New York: Alfred A. Knopf, Inc., 1953.

Fling, Fred M. *The Writing of History: An Introduction to Historical Method.* New Haven: The Yale University Press, 1920.

Garraghan, Gilbert J. *A Guide to Historical Method.* Edited by Jean Delanglez. New York: Fordham University Press, 1956.
   A very scholarly, advanced guide.

Geyl, Pieter. *The Use and Abuse of History.* New Haven: The Yale University Press, 1955.

Gray, Wood, *et al. Historian's Handbook.* 2nd ed. Boston: Houghton Mifflin Company, 1964.
   Contains good basic bibliographies for all fields of historical inquiry.

Gustavson, Carl. *A Preface to History.* New York: McGraw-Hill, 1955.
   An extremely enlightening work—quite suitable for the beginning student.

Hexter, J. H. *Reappraisals in History.* New York: Harper & Row, Publishers, 1961.

Hockett, Homer C. *The Critical Method in Historical Research and Writing.* New York: The Macmillan Company, 1955.

Kent, Sherman. *Writing History,* 2nd ed. New York: Appleton-Century-Crofts, 1967.

Lucey, William L. *History: Methods and Interpretation.* Chicago: Loyola University Press, 1958.

Nevins, Allan. *Gateway to History.* rev. ed. Boston: D. C. Heath, 1962.

Renier, Gustaf. *History: Its Purpose and Method.* Boston: The Beacon Press, 1950.

Saveth, Edward N. (ed.). *American History and the Social Sciences.* Glencoe, Illinois: The Free Press, 1964.
   Describes the natural integration of the various disciplines.

2. WORKS ON PHILOSOPHY OF HISTORY

Barraclough, Geoffrey. *History in a Changing World.* Oxford: The Blackwell Press, 1955.

Cairns, Grace E. *Philosophies of History: Meeting of East and West in Cycle-Pattern Theories of History.* New York: Philosophical Library, 1962.

Carr, Edward H. *What Is History?* New York: Alfred A. Knopf, Inc., 1962.

Childe, V. Gordon. *What Is History?* New York: H. Schuman Company, 1953.

Collingwood, R. C. *The Idea of History.* Oxford: The Clarendon Press, 1946.

D'Arcy, Martin C. *The Sense of History.* London: Faber and Faber, 1959.

Dray, William H. *Philosophy of History.* Englewood Cliffs, New Jersey: Prentice-Hall, Inc., 1964.
   A good survey of the various approaches.

Gardiner, Patrick (ed.). *Theories of History.* Glencoe, Illinois: The Free Press, 1959.

Gottschalk, Louis. *Understanding History.* New York: Alfred A. Knopf, Inc., 1950.

Klibansky, Raymond, and Paton, H. J. (eds.). *Philosophy and History: Essays Presented to Ernst Cassirer.* New York: Harper & Row, Publishers, 1963.

Lowith, Karl. *Meaning in History: The Theological Implications of the Philosophy of History.* Chicago: The University of Chicago Press, 1959.

Malin, J. C. *On the Nature of History: Essays About History and Dissidence.* Lawrence, Kansas: By the Author, 1954.

Muller, Herbert J. *The Uses of the Past: Profiles of Former Societies.* New York: Oxford University Press, 1952.

Ortega y Gasset, Jose. *History as a System: And Other Essays Toward a Philosophy of History.* New York: W. W. Norton & Company, Inc., 1961.

Pieper, Josef. *The End of Time: A Meditation on the Philosophy of History.* Translated by M. Bulloch. New York: Pantheon Books, 1954.

Rowse, A. L. *The Use of History.* New York: The Macmillan Company, 1947.

Russell, Bertrand. *Understanding History and Other Essays.* New York: Philosophical Library, 1957.

Stern, F. *The Varieties of History.* Cleveland: World Publishing Company, 1956.

Strayer, Joseph R. (ed.). *The Interpretation of History.* Princeton: Princeton University Press, 1943. Reprinted New York: Peter Smith, 1950.

Teggart, Frederick J. *Theory and Processes in History.* Berkeley: University of California Press, 1941.

3. GUIDE TO BIBLIOGRAPHIES

The bibliographies contained in this section pertain only to works written in the English language. Further information may be found in Nevins' *Gateway to History.* Listed below are basic bibliographies for all geographical divisions of history, including foreign language works, excellent bibliographies contained in the Langer series, the Bibliography of British History series, and the older Cambridge historical series.

American Catalogue of Books, 1876–1910. New York: Publishers Weekly, 1881–1911.

Annual American Catalogue, 1886–1910. New York: Publishers Weekly, 1887–1911.

Beers, Henry P. *Bibliographies in American History.* rev. ed. New York: The H. W. Wilson Company, 1942.

    The work contains over 11,000 indexed entries.

Bemis, Samuel F., and Griffin, Grace G. *Guide to the Diplomatic History of the United States, 1775–1921.* Washington: Government Printing Office, 1935.

Besterman, Theodore. *A World Bibliography of Bibliographies.* 3rd ed. Geneva: Societas Bibliographica, 1955–1956.

Billington, Ray A. *Westward Expansion.* 2nd ed. New York: The Macmillan Company, 1960.

    Although this is a textbook, its bibliography warrants its inclusion here.

Cambridge Ancient History, The. 12 vols. New York: The Macmillan Company, 1923–1939.

The Cambridge series possesses extensive chapter bibliographies.

Cambridge Bibliography of English Literature, 600–1900. 5 vols. New York: The Macmillan Company, 1941–1957.

Cambridge Medieval History, The. 8 vols. New York: The Macmillan Company, 1911–1936.

Cambridge Modern History, The. 13 vols. New York: The Macmillan Company, 1902–1926.

Catalogue of Printed Books in the Library of the British Museum. 95 vols. London: William Clowes and Sons, Ltd., 1881–1900. Supplement, 1900–1905. 15 vols.

> *General Catalogue of Printed Books.* 51 vols. 1934–1956, carries the series forward.

Channing, Edward, Hart, Albert, and Turner, Frederick J. *Guide to the Study and Reading of American History.* rev. ed. Boston: Ginn and Company, 1912.

> The work covers what had been written up to 1910 and is consequently not up to date, but it has been superseded by the *Harvard Guide* listed below.

Clark, G. N. (ed.). *The Oxford History of England.* 14 vols. New York: Oxford University Press, 1934–1961.

Cumulative Book Index. New York: The H. W. Wilson Company, 1898—.

> Lists everything written in the English language and published anywhere in the world.

Cuthbertson, Stuart, and Ewers, John. *A Preliminary Bibliography of the American Fur Trade.* St. Louis: Jefferson National Expansion Memorial, 1938.

> The work is of much broader scope than the title would indicate.

English Catalogue of Books, 1801—. London: Publisher's Circular, 1837—.

> Now published quarterly.

Evans, Charles. *American Bibliography, 1639–1820.* 13 vols. Chicago: The Blakely Press, 1903–1934.

> The work is indexed.

Gohdes, Clarence L. *Bibliographical Guide to the Study of the Literature of the U.S.A.* Durham, North Carolina: Duke University Press, 1959.

Griffin, A. P., comp. *Bibliography of American Historical Societies.* Washington: Government Printing Office, 1907.

> Originally the Report of the American Historical Association for 1905.

Handlin, Oscar, *et al. Harvard Guide to American History.* Cambridge: Harvard University Press, 1954.

> Covers the period up to 1950.

Howe, George F. *Guide to Historical Literature.* New York: The Macmillan Company, 1961.

International Index: A Guide to Periodical Literature in the Social Sciences and Humanities. New York: The H. W. Wilson Company, 1907—.

> Kept up to date with quarterly supplements.

Jones, Howard M. *Guide to American Literature and Its Backgrounds Since 1890.* 2nd rev. ed. Cambridge: Harvard University Press, 1959.

Kelly, James. *American Catalogue of Books Published in the United States from January 1861 to January 1871.* 2 vols. New York: Wiley Company, 1866–1871.

Langer, William L. (ed.). *The Rise of Modern Europe.* 20 vols. New York: Harper & Row, 1934—.

Matthews, William, and Pearce, Roy. *American Diaries: An Annotated Bibliography of American Diaries Written Prior to the Year 1861.* Berkeley: University of California Press, 1945.

National Union Catalogue. 28 vols. Ann Arbor: Edwards Company, 1958.
Covers the years 1953–1957 and includes works that are not listed in the Library of Congress publications noted below.

New York Times Index. New York Times, 1913.

Paetow, Louis J. *A Guide to the Study of Medieval History.* rev. ed. New York: F. S. Crofts and Company, 1931.

Poole's Index to Periodical Literature, 1802–1881. rev. ed. 2 vols. Boston: Houghton Mifflin Company, 1891.
Supplements carry the work to 1906.

Ragatz, Lowell. *A Bibliography for the Study of European History, 1815–1939.* Ann Arbor: Edwards Brothers, 1942.

Reader's Guide to Periodical Literature. New York: The H. W. Wilson Company, 1900—.
Issued monthly and bound annually.

Reed, Conoyers. *Bibliography of British History: Tudor Period, 1485–1603.* 2nd ed. Oxford: Clarendon Press, 1959.
Other volumes are in process to bring the series forward by historical period.

Roorback, Orville. *Bibliotheca Americana, 1820–1861.* 4 vols. New York: A. O. Roorback, 1852–1861.
Arranged in alphabetical order.

Sabine, Joseph, *et al. Dictionary of Books Relating to America from Its Discovery to the Present Time.* 29 vols. New York: J. Sabine, 1868–1936.
Lists more than 106,000 items.

United States Catalogue, 1900—. Marion E. Potter, *et al.,* eds. New York: The H. W. Wilson Company, 1900—.

United States, Library of Congress. *Catalogue of Books Represented By Library of Congress Printed Cards.* 167 vols. Ann Arbor: Edwards Company, 1942–1946.
Covers the period 1898–1942.
Supplement. 42 vols. Ann Arbor: Edwards Company, 1948.
Covers the years 1942–1947.

United States, Library of Congress. *The Library of Congress Author Catalogue.* 24 vols. Ann Arbor: Edwards Company, 1953.
Covers the years 1948–1952.

United States, Library of Congress. *The Library of Congress, Books: Subjects.* 20 vols. Ann Arbor: Edwards Company, 1955. Covers the period 1950–1954. Additional coverage by a different publishing house as follows:
22 vols. Patterson, New Jersey: Pageant Books, 1961.
Covers the years 1955–1959.

Winchell, Constance (ed.). *Guide to Reference Books.* 7th ed. Chicago: American Library Association, 1951.
First edition appeared in 1930.

4. WRITINGS ON AMERICAN HISTORY

Griffin, Grace G. *Writings on American History, 1906–1940.* Volumes for different years are published by different companies as follows:
1906–1908—3 vols. New York: The Macmillan Company, 1908–1910.
1909–1911—3 vols. Washington: Government Printing Office, 1911–1913.
1912–1917—6 vols. New Haven: Yale University Press, 1914–1919.
1918–1940—21 vols. American Historical Association, *Annual Report.*
McLaughlin, Andrew C., *et al. Writings on American History, 1903.* Washington: The Carnegie Institution, 1905.
Masterson, James E. *Writings on American History, 1948—.* American Historical Association, *Annual Report.*
Richardson, Ernest, and Anson, Ely. *Writings on American History, 1902.* Princeton: Library Bookstore, 1904.
Despite the work accomplished by individuals and under the sanction of the American Historical Association, there still remain gaps for 1904–1905 and 1941–1947.

5. BASIC REFERENCE WORKS

Barnhart, Clarence L., and Halsey, William D. (eds.). *The New Century Cyclopedia of Names.* 3 vols. New York: Appleton-Century-Crofts, Inc., 1954.
Book Review Digest, 1905—. New York: The H. W. Wilson Company, 1905—.
Langer, William, and Gatzke, Hans (eds.). *An Encyclopedia of World History, Ancient, Medieval, and Modern, Chronologically Arranged.* rev. ed. Boston: Houghton Mifflin Company, 1956.
Morris, Richard B. (ed.). *Encyclopedia of American History.* New York: Harper & Brothers, Publishers, 1953.
Palmer, Robert, *et al. Atlas of World History.* Chicago: Rand McNally & Company, 1957.
Pauk, Walter. *How to Study in College.* Boston: Houghton Mifflin Company, 1962.
Paullin, Charles O. *Atlas of the Historical Geography of the United States.* New York: American Geographical Society, 1932.
Pugh, Griffith T. *Guide to Research Writing.* 2nd ed. Boston: Houghton Mifflin Company, 1963.
Strong on bibliographical entry and footnote citation.
Roeder, William S. *Dictionary of European History.* New York: Philosophical Library, 1954.
Spiller, Robert, *et al. Literary History of the United States.* New York: The Macmillan Company, 1948.

Turabian, Kate L. *A Manual for Writers of Term Papers, Theses, and Dissertations.* rev. ed. Chicago: The University of Chicago Press, 1955.

United States, Library of Congress. *A Guide to the Study of the United States of America.* Washington: Government Printing Office, 1960.

United States, Library of Congress, General Reference and Bibliography Division. *List of National Archives Microfilms.* Washington: Government Printing Office, 1961.
> Constantly being revised—covers period from 1940 forward.

6. BIOGRAPHICAL GUIDES

Biography Index. New York: The H. W. Wilson Company, 1946—.
> Supplemented monthly by *Current Biography.* New York: The H. W. Wilson Company.

Cattell, Jacques (ed.). *Dictionary of American Scholars.* Lancaster, Pennsylvania: The Science Press, 1951.

Cyclopaedia of American Biography, The. new enl. ed. 6 vols. New York: Press Associates, Compilers, Inc., 1915.
> This work is commonly referred to as "Appleton's Cyclopedia."

Johnson, Allen, and Malone, Dumas (eds.). *Dictionary of American Biography.* 22 vols. New York: Charles Scribner's Sons, 1928–1944.
> Supplements continue the work.

Who Was Who. 2 vols. Chicago: The Marcus Company, 1942–1950.

Who's Who in America. Chicago: Marcus Who's Who, Inc., 1899—. Published biennially from 1899 to 1939. Monthly supplements begin in 1939.

7. GUIDES TO PUBLISHED GOVERNMENT DOCUMENTS

A. *Records of the Congress in Chronological Order*

Ford, W. C., and Hunt, Gaillard (eds.). *Journals of the Continental Congresses, 1774–1789.* 34 vols. Washington: Government Printing Office, 1904–1907.

Debates and Proceedings in the Congress of the United States, 1789–1824. 42 vols. Washington: Government Printing Office, 1834–1856.
> Compiled by Gales and Seaton, this portion of the records of Congress is usually referred to as the *Annals of Congress.*

Register of Debates in Congress, Containing the Debates and Proceedings, 1825–1837. 29 vols. Washington: Gales and Seaton, editors and publishers, 1825–1837.

Congressional Globe, Containing the Debates and Proceedings, 1833–1873. 109 vols. Washington: F. P. Blair, *et al.,* editors and publishers, 1834–1873.

Congressional Record, Containing the Debates and Proceedings, 1873—. Washington: Government Printing Office, 1873—.

B. *Materials on Foreign Affairs Arranged Chronologically*

Wharton, Francis. *The Revolutionary Diplomatic Correspondence of the United States.* 6 vols. Washington: Blair and Rives, 1889.

American State Papers, Foreign Relations, Class I, 1789–1828. Washington: Lowrie, Gales, and Seaton, editors and publishers.

Hasse, Adelaide R. *Index to United States Documents Relating to Foreign Affairs, 1828–1861.* 3 vols. Washington: The Carnegie Institution, 1914–1921.

United States, Department of State. *General Index to the Published Volumes of the Diplomatic Correspondence of the United States, 1861–1899.* Washington: Government Printing Office, 1902.

United States, Department of State. *Papers Relating to the Foreign Relations of the United States, 1861—.* Washington: Government Printing Office. The series has now reached the 1930's.

United States, Department of State. *Papers Relating to the Foreign Relations of the United States: General Index, 1900–1918.* Washington: Government Printing Office, 1946.
No further indices have been prepared.

Miller, Hunter (ed.). *Treaties and Other International Acts of the United States of America.* Washington: Government Printing Office, 1948.
Continues the *Foreign Relations,* but on a more selected basis.

C. *Miscellaneous Government References*

Boyd, Anne M. *United States Government Publications.* New York: The H. W. Wilson Company, 1949.

Farrand, Max (ed.). *The Records of the First Federal Convention of 1787.* 4 vols. New Haven: Yale University Press, 1911.

Hirshberg, H. S., and Melinat, C. H. *Subject Guide to United States Government Publications.* Chicago: American Library Association, 1947.

Statutes at Large of the United States, 1789–1873. 17 vols. Boston: Little, Brown, 1845–1873.

Statutes at Large of the United States, 1873—. Washington: Government Printing Office, 1875—.

8. WORKS ON HISTORIOGRAPHY

Anderson, E. N., and Cate, J. L. (eds.). *Medieval and Historiographical Essays in Honor of James Westfall Thompson.* Chicago: The University of Chicago Press, 1938.

Ausubel, Herman, *et al.* (eds.). *Some Modern Historians of Britain.* New York: The Dryden Press, 1951.

Barnes, Harry E. *A History of Historical Writing.* rev. ed. New York: Dover Publications, 1961.
First published at Norman: University of Oklahoma Press, 1937.

Bassett, John S. *The Middle Group of American Historians*. New York: The Macmillan Company, 1917.

Bellot, Hugh H. *American History and American Historians*. London: The Athlone Press, 1952.

Engel-Janase, Friedrich. *The Growth of German Historicism*. Baltimore: Johns Hopkins Press, 1954.

Ferguson, W. K. *The Renaissance in Historical Thought*. New York: Houghton Mifflin Company, 1948.

Fitzsimons, Matthew, Pundt, Alfred, and Nowell, Charles (eds.). *The Development of Historiography*. Harrisburg, Pennsylvania: The Stackpole Company, 1954.

Gooch, George P. *History and Historians in the 19th Century*. 2nd ed. London: Longmans, Green, 1913.
Reprinted New York: Peter Smith, 1949.
Covers mainly European historiography but is good on American also.

Halperin, S. William. *Some Twentieth-Century Historians*. Chicago: University of Chicago Press, 1961.

Higham, John, Gilbert, Felix, and Krieger, Leonard. *History*. Englewood Cliffs, New Jersey: Prentice-Hall, Inc., 1965.
Compares European and American historiography—surveys modern trends.

Historical Scholarship in America: Needs and Opportunities. New York: American Historical Association, 1932.

Hutchinson, William T. (ed.). *The Marcus W. Jernegan Essays in American Historiography*. Chicago: The University of Chicago Press, 1937.

Jameson, J. Franklin. *The History of Historical Writings in America*. Boston: Houghton Mifflin Company, 1891.
A classic work but now considerably out of date.

Kraus, Michael. *The Writing of American History*. Norman: University of Oklahoma Press, 1953.
The beginning student is strongly encouraged to prepare for his historical readings by studying this work.

Levin, David. *History as Romantic Art: Bancroft, Prescott, Motely, and Parkman*. Stanford: Stanford University Press, 1959.

Neff, E. *The Poetry of History*. New York: Columbia University Press, 1947.

Powicke, F. M. *Modern Historians and the Study of History*. London: The Odhams Press, 1955.

Robinson, James H. *The New History*. New York: The Macmillan Company, 1916.

Sanders, Jennings B. *Historical Interpretations and American Historianship*. Yellow Springs, Ohio: Antioch Press, 1966.

Schmitt, Bernadotte (ed.). *Some Historians of Modern Europe*. Chicago: The University of Chicago Press, 1942.

Sheehan, Donald H., and Syrett, Harold C. (eds.). *Essays in American Historiography: Papers Presented in Honor of Allan Nevins*. New York: Columbia University Press, 1960.

Shotwell, James T. *The History of History*. Vol. I. New York: Columbia University Press, 1939.
This ambitious work is intended to survey the entire course of historical

writings throughout the history of civilization. Only the first volume, pertaining to ancient history, has appeared.

Thompson, James W., and Holm, Bernard J. *A History of Historical Writing.* 2 vols. New York: The Macmillan Company, 1942.

Wish, Harvey. *The American Historian: A Social-Intellectual History of the Writing of the American Past.* New York: Oxford University Press, 1960.

9. RELATED ARTICLES IN PROFESSIONAL JOURNALS

Beale, Howard K. "What Historians Have Said About the Causes of the Civil War," *Theory and Practice in Historical Study: A Report of the Committee on Historiography.* New York: Social Science Research Council, 1946.

Binkley, William C. "Two World Wars and American Historical Scholarship," *Mississippi Valley Historical Review.* XXXIII (June 1946).

Boyd, J. P. "State and Local Historical Societies in the United States," *American Historical Review.* XL (1934), pp. 10–37.

Ellis, Elmer. "The Profession of Historian," *Mississippi Valley Historical Review.* XXXVIII (1951), pp. 3–20.

Hempel, Carl G. "The Function of General Laws in History," *Journal of Philosophy.* XXXIX (1942), pp. 35–48.

"History and Historiography," *Encyclopedia of the Social Sciences.* 15 vols. New York: Encyclopedia of the Social Sciences, 1930–1935, VII.

Iggers, Georg G. "The Idea of Progress in Recent Philosophies of History," *Journal of Modern History.* XXX (1958), pp. 215–226.

Jameson, J. Franklin. "The Future Uses of History," *American Historical Review.* LXV (1950), pp. 61–72.

Link, Arthur S. "A Decade of Biographical Contributions to Recent American History," *Mississippi Valley Historical Review.* XXXIV (1947), pp. 637–642.

McMurtrie, Donald. "Locating the Printed Source Materials for United States History, with a Bibliography of Lists of Regional Imprints," *Mississippi Valley Historical Review.* XXXI (1944), pp. 369–378.

Nowell, Charles E. "Has the Past a Place in History?" *Journal of Modern History.* XXIV (1952), pp. 331–340.

Ross, E. D. "A Generation of Prairie Historiography," *Mississippi Valley Historical Review.* XXXIII (1946), pp. 391–410.

Schindler, Margaret C. "Fictitious Biography," *American Historical Review.* XLII (1937), pp. 680–690.

Sears, Lawrence. "The Meaning of History," *Journal of Philosophy.* XXXIX (1942), pp. 393–401.

Simkhovitch, Vladimir. "Approaches to History," *Political Science Quarterly.* XLIV (1929), pp. 481–498.

———. "Approaches to History," *Political Science Quarterly.* XLV (1930), pp. 481–527.

Smith, Goldwin. "The Treatment of History," *American Historical Review.* X (1905), pp. 511–520.

Smith, Theodore C. "The Writing of American History in America from 1884 to 1934," *American Historical Review.* XL (1935), pp. 439–449.

10. SELECTED LIST OF PROFESSIONAL JOURNALS

What follows is a representative listing of the various types of professional historical journals currently being published. These journals are particularly important for two reasons: one, they contain many worthwhile professional book reviews, and two, they contain many monographic articles possessing a degree of detail not found in the ordinary textbook.

Since this is only a representative list, the reader is directed to the following sources for detailed and thorough listings of all professional historical publications.

Boehm, Eric, and Lalit, Adolphus. *Historical Periodicals: An Annotated World List of Historical and Related Serial Publications.* Santa Barbara, California: The Clio Press, 1961.

Caron, Pierre, and Jaryc, Marc. *World List of Historical Periodicals.* New York: The H. W. Wilson Company, 1939.

American Archivist.
American Historical Review.
American Jewish Historical Quarterly.
American Political Science Review.
American Scholar.
Annals of the Association of American Geographers.
Business History Review.
Canadian Historical Review.
Catholic Historical Review.
Economic History Review.
English History Review.
Far Eastern Quarterly.
Hispanic American Historical Review.
Historical Bulletin.
Historical Outlook.
History of Education Quarterly.
Journal of American History—formerly the *Mississippi Valley Historical Review.*
Journal of Church and State.
Journal of Modern History.
Journal of Negro History.
Journal of Southern History.
Journal of the History of Ideas.
Library of Congress Quarterly Journal.
Middle East Journal.
New England Quarterly.
New York Times Book Review.
Pacific Historical Review.
Political Science Quarterly.
Proceedings of the American Philosophical Society.
Slavic Review.
Southwestern Social Science Quarterly.

GLOSSARY OF HISTORICAL TERMS

APPENDIX **B**

The terms that are defined below are often used in both classroom and textbook but are not always defined. The list is not a definitive list because history is not possessed of a special language. However, many expressions that are used in history are not normally used in everyday language.

ABSOLUTISM   Term pertaining to a ruler or government possessing complete power and authority over the people. As contrasted with limited power under a constitutional system.

ADMIRALITY COURT   A court that has primary jurisdiction over maritime issues, i.e., tariffs, port taxes, licenses, contraband, and seagoing violations.

AMBASSADOR   The diplomatic agents of any country who operate at the highest level. They are superior to lower level diplomatic agents, such as consuls.

ANARCHISM   An extremist theory which holds that all forms of government tyrannize mankind and therefore must be destroyed. Commonly pertains to lawlessness.

ANNEXATION   The incorporation or addition of territories into the boundaries of an existing nation.

ANTE BELLUM   Latin term signifying the period before a war. Commonly used with reference to the American Civil War, e.g., the ante bellum South.

APPEASEMENT   Diplomatic policy of nations to give in to strong demands from a powerful nation in order to avert the possibility of war.

ARBITRATION   The settlement of a dispute between nations by a person or group mutually chosen by the disputants for this purpose.

ARCHIVES   The written records of a government, or any other organization, which are stored away in the "dead letter" file.

ARISTOCRACY   Term applied to the privileged upper class, the nobility, which possesses political, social, and economic rights not accorded to the mass of the people.

ARMISTICE The suspension of military operations by all parties concerned according to a mutually agreed upon set of arrangements. Usually is the preface to a peace treaty, whereas a truce is only a temporary cessation of hostilities.

AUTONOMY Term signifying the self-governing or independent status of a nation-state.

BALANCE OF POWER An alliance structure, which results in equal strength for all major potential combatants, thereby acting as a deterrent to military operations.

BELLIGERENT A nation engaging in war and recognized as such by several or all other nations.

BENEVOLENT DESPOT A ruler who governs his subjects in an absolute manner, but who has the welfare of his subjects at heart and works toward this goal.

BLOCKADE The cutting off of normal trade and communications channels of a nation by another nation through the use of military and naval forces.

BOURGEOISIE Term applied to describe the European middle class and the values of that class. Originally, it applied to "burgers," i.e., townsmen.

BUFFER STATE An independent nation or territory strategically located between potential belligerent powers, which tends to act as security for one or both of these powers against attack.

BULLION (HARD MONEY) That medium of exchange which is in the form of gold and silver, not paper currency or credit slips. Used mainly in international payments and trade deficits.

CABAL An obsolescent term once used to signify a plot or conspiracy, usually against a government.

CANON LAW The rules and regulations of a religious organization, most often used with reference to the Catholic Church. However, a "canon" applies to the laws of any religious governing body.

CAPITALISM An economic system based on private property ownership, the wage system, individual initiative, competition, and the profit motive.

CAUSUS BELLI A Latin term used in diplomatic history, which refers to the causes or justification for going to war.

CLERICALISM The influencing of political matters by the clergy of a given religious institution—a political system that upholds the political power of the clergy.

COLLECTIVE SECURITY The attempt to maintain world or regional peace through the combined efforts of nations, e.g., the Concert of Europe, the United Nations, the Organization of American States, etc.

COMMUNISM Theoretically, an economic system based on public ownership of the means of production, with profits being shared by all members of the society. Eventually results in the abolition of class and government. However, in practice it is usually associated with totalitarianism, inequality, and lack of freedom.

CONCILIARISM The movement in the medieval church forward, which held that a general church council was superior to the rulings of the Popes—a revolt against traditional religious authority.

CONFEDERATION A political organization consisting of a union of sovereign political bodies for specific purposes only. Real power resides in the member nations. Contrast with federation.

CONSERVATISM An individual or governmental attitude that is opposed to changes in policy or organization. Prefers to either maintain the status quo, or reestablish an older, less liberal scheme of things.

CONSTITUTIONALISM Government based on an agreement between the people and their rulers, either written or unwritten, establishing the limits of power and the duties of that government.

CONTRABAND Articles that are considered by belligerents to be necessary for the war effort. Originally, contraband referred to munitions only; later, it included foodstuffs, clothing, etc. Contraband articles in shipments by neutral nations may be seized by belligerents if they are destined for other belligerents.

CONVENTION A treaty of a specific nature, which is usually agreed to by many nations concurrently.

COUP D'ETAT The sudden and violent overthrow of any existing government by a militant minority.

DARWINISM The theory of evolution which holds that creatures survive and improve by adapting to environmental changes. Results in "survival of the fittest," a basic doctrine used by nations in both domestic and foreign policy.

DE FACTO Pertains to a government which actually exists (usually after a revolution) but which is not yet recognized as legitimate or stable by other established nations.

DE JURE Pertains to any government recognized as legitimate by other nations, even though it may not be actually functioning, e.g., a government in exile during wartime.

DEPRESSION (PANIC) A period in a business cycle marked by lower wages, unemployment, and declining profits. Compare with a panic, which is a sudden and very serious depression, or with a recession, which is a relatively mild depression.

DOMINION A self-governing independent and sovereign nation within the British imperial system. Present-day ties are based primarily on tradition and respect for the English monarchy.

DYNASTY Term used to describe the hereditary, ruling family of a nation. Also the name given to the historical period when a particular ruling house holds power.

EMBARGO Trade restrictions placed by a nation on international commerce. May only pertain to a particular nation or a single commodity. Usually resorted to as a coercive measure.

ENTENTE An understanding on important international matters between several nations jointly.

EVOLUTION A gradual and peaceful change in the organizational structure of any facet of a society, as contrasted with the sudden changes characterized by a revolution.

EXTRATERRITORIALITY The right or privilege of a person to be tried under his own legal system, even when residing on alien territory, e.g., China, ca. 1900.

FASCISM A totalitarian, suppressive governmental system glorifying nationalism, militarism, and racism while suppressing individual liberties. Its major difference from totalitarian communism is the presence of private ownership of the means of production, but under very rigid government control.

FEDERATION   A union of sovereign political bodies that give up most or all of their sovereignty to create an overriding superior governing body of permanent stature, e.g., the United States.

FEUDALISM   Institution in medieval European and comparable Japanese history whereby individuals held land and political power from their rulers in exchange for political support and military service.

FREEDOM OF THE SEAS   The right of the seagoing merchant vessels of any nation to travel freely and equally on the high seas.

FREE SHIPS MAKE FREE GOODS   The international theory that the nonmilitary goods of a belligerent are free from seizure by other belligerents when being transported upon the vessels of a neutral nation.

FREE TRADE ASSOCIATION   An agreement reached between several countries, abolishing any trade restrictions among the signers. Seeks to further the free flow of goods across international boundaries and is ultimately aimed at the complete abolition of all tariffs.

GENTLEMAN'S AGREEMENT   An understanding between national leaders, the enforcement of which rests on the good word of the parties involved.

GUILD SYSTEM   Medieval organization of individuals employed in a certain craft to establish training requirements, business practices, and mutual protection of the members.

HAGIOGRAPHY   The study and writing that is concerned with the lives of saintly historical figures.

HERETIC (HERESY)   A person who upholds doctrines opposing the official teachings of a religious body; any teaching that runs contrary to the official teachings of such a body.

HOLDING COMPANY (POOL)   A business organization created to hold the stocks of many producing companies, the purpose of which is to control the prices and behavior of these companies in the direction of monopoly.

ICONOCLASM   The policy of attacking and destroying the traditional venerated objects, institutions, and doctrines of a religious body.

IMPERIALISM   That policy engaged in by a nation seeking to expand its boundaries and its sphere of political control at the expense of other, weaker nations.

IMPRESSMENT   The policy of strong naval nations, particularly early modern England, to forcibly press individuals into naval service, often by removing them from the vessels of other nations.

INSURRECTION (INSURGENCY)   A rebellion against established authority; may take the form of bloody civil conflict or may simply be the refusal of a politician to follow the dictates of his party's leadership.

INTERNATIONAL LAW   Those principles that a majority of civilized nations agree to respect in their intercourse with one another.

ISOLATIONISM   The policy of a nation to avoid any entangling dealings with other nations; a tendency to look inward, as contrasted with internationalism.

JINGOISTIC   Sword-rattling—a militant, warlike stand in foreign policy.

LETTER OF MARQUE   The official, written sanction by a government to private individuals, empowering them to engage in privateering, i.e., attack enemy shipping at their own expense, and to share the profits with the monarch.

LIBERALISM   A relative term currently denoting an individual or governmental attitude that favors changes in the existing structure in the direction of greater governmental power to be used to further individual freedom and to provide greater services for the mass of the people. Can also refer to more democratic government and basic political reform as in nineteenth-century England.

MANDATE   Territory governed by an advanced nation at the request and sanction of a governing body of nations.

MANOR   The territories held by a lord from his king, over which he exercises authority and which he subdivides into parcels to be worked by his serfs— the economic side of feudalism.

MERCANTILISM   A political-economic theory whereby a nation seeks self-sufficiency through the accumulation of gold and silver by means of a favorable balance of trade and by colonies used as sources for raw materials and markets.

MERCENARY   A professional soldier who would sell his services to the army of any nation strictly for pay. Most commonly employed prior to the nineteenth century.

MOBILIZATION   To make ready the armed forces of a nation for battle, primarily before the days of large standing armies. Usually was a rather lengthy process and was regarded as an aggressive measure.

MODUS VIVENDI   A temporary agreement between nations, which is only in force until a final settlement is reached.

MONASTICISM   Pertains to the system in which religious men and women retire from the world to a cloistered existence, i.e., a monastery, nunnery, or convent, and live a permanent, communal, religious life.

MONOGRAPH   An article or a book written about one specific subject only— as contrasted with a general textbook.

MORATORIUM   The temporary suspension of payments due for debts by common consent of creditor and debtor. Usually refers to debtor nation, e.g., the moratorium on war debts in 1930.

MOST-FAVORED-NATION THEORY   Agreement between two nations stating that they will give no other nation greater commercial privileges than they grant to each other.

NATIONALISM   That attitude or feeling emphasizing loyalty and patriotism toward one's country by a national group, i.e., one with common language, an accepted heritage, and well-defined, more or less permanent boundaries.

NEUTRALITY   The diplomatic policy whereby a nation refrains from getting involved in any way in a war between other nations—to be strictly impartial.

OLIGARCHY   Governmental rule by an aristocratic minority. As contrasted with a dictatorship (rule by one) and a democracy (rule by the majority).

OPEN DOOR   Term used to symbolize the policy of equal opportunities of nations in their international commercial dealings.

OSTRACISM   The policy of ejecting or punishing an individual in a given society by completely ignoring his presence. Used in the ancient world and by the American Indian, among others.

PACIFISM   The attitude holding that all force is morally wrong and must be peaceably opposed, e.g., war is wrong; therefore, resist the draft or any national policy that involves warfare.

PALEOGRAPHY   Pertains to the study and interpretation of obsolete handwritings to determine authenticity and ownership.

PAPAL BULL   A formal pronouncement on the teachings and interpretations of the Catholic Church as formulated by the Pope.

PAPER BLOCKADE   A blockade that is declared but is nonenforceable due to the lack of sufficient military strength. Usually not considered binding by other nations.

PARITY   Term normally pertaining to farm prices. It is the ratio of the value of money at a given time to its value at a given base period, e.g., the value of farm prices in 1900 compared to the average of prices for the years 1880–1890.

PATRONAGE   The power on the part of a politician to appoint various individuals to public offices, usually as a reward for political support.

PLEBISCITE   A popular vote by the people in a given area on major political issues, primarily used to determine independent status or choice of government.

POSITIVISM   A philosophical system based on empirical knowledge (positive sense perception)—quite prominent from August Comte forward.

POST BELLUM   Latin term standing for the period immediately following a war.

PRAGMATISM   A philosophical system emphasizing the determination of the validity of an idea by whether or not it actually works. Has a tendency to result in relative morality.

PRIMOGENITURE   The feudalistic European practice of the father's estate being passed on undivided to the eldest son, to prevent the fragmentation of political and economic power.

PROGRESSIVISM   The favoring of progress through a program of social and political reform—the realization of Lockean natural rights through the use of the strong, centralized government concept of Alexander Hamilton.

PROTECTIVE TARIFF   The levying of import duties that are sufficiently high so as to prevent the importation of foreign goods, thereby protecting domestic industry from foreign competition.

PROTECTORATE   A weak or small nation over which some strong nation assumes protection, usually concerning foreign affairs and usually with some strings attached.

PROVISIONAL GOVERNMENT   A temporary government established to provide law and order pending the final determination of a permanent form of government—usually exists immediately after a revolution.

RADICAL   One who favors extreme change of the basic political and/or social system; considerably beyond the objectives of the liberal.

RAPPROCHEMENT   Term used to describe the establishment of satisfactory relations—the settling of an outstanding, major dispute.

RATIFICATION   The formal acceptance, by the proper consenting authority, of an act of government. May be the people accepting a new constitution, the

Senate accepting a treaty, the States accepting a constitutional amendment, etc.

REACTIONARY One who is an extreme conservative and seeks to counteract any progressive acts; retrenchive—exists primarily during periods of unrest.

RECIPROCITY (RECIPROCAL TRADE/RECIPROCAL TARIFF) The granting of favorable commercial benefits to a nation with the condition that the other nation responds in equal manner.

RECONSTRUCTION The process of rebuilding an area or a nation following a devastating war, e.g., post-Civil War South, or "reconstruction" loans to the Allies following World War I.

REPARATIONS Payments made by a defeated nation following a war for damages inflicted on civilian property and lives. May be made in money, in goods, or in labor.

REVENUE TARIFF The levying of import duties that are sufficiently low so as not to curtail the importation of foreign goods but rather to obtain revenues from the duties imposed on the goods.

REVOLUTION The usually violent and sudden overthrow of an existing government. May be bloody, e.g., the French Revolution, or may be quite peaceful, e.g., the English Revolution of 1688.

SCHISM The disunion of an organized group (society, church, political party, etc.) because of differences in opinion on basic doctrines or beliefs. Usually applied to the fragmentation of Christianity.

SELF-DETERMINATION The right of the people residing in a given area to determine for themselves their form of government. Implies sovereignty.

SHIRT-SLEEVE DIPLOMACY Pertains to diplomatic relations of the informal type. Sometimes connotes crude diplomatic dealings.

SOCIALISM An economic system calling for public ownership and operation of the means of production, and the subsequent sharing of profits. An attempt to equalize the distribution of wealth through social welfare programs and graduated tax measures.

SOFT MONEY Term used by silver currency advocates who oppose a paper currency backed by gold.

SOVEREIGNTY That characteristic of a nation rendering it truly independent and supreme over its territories and people.

STATUS QUO The maintenance of conditions exactly as they exist—with no changes.

STATUS QUO ANTE BELLUM Diplomatic term used to describe a peace or armistice based on conditions as they existed before hostilities began.

TENURE Term pertaining to the length or duration of an office held by a public official.

TOTALITARIANISM A governmental system in which one party or a small group possesses complete control and declares all opposition to be illegal.

TRUCE A temporary cessation of hostilities between belligerents, which does not provide the groundwork for permanent peace—not to be confused with armistice.

TYRANT One who rules not only absolutely, i.e., a dictator, but who also rules oppressively and cruelly.

UTOPIA (UTOPIAN)   An imaginary place or age where everything exists in a perfect state. Any attempt to create a perfect social or political system.

VISIT AND SEARCH   The right of a belligerent to stop, board, and search a neutral merchant vessel on the high seas to determine if it might be carrying contraband.

CHRONOLOGICAL TABLES

This unit contains three major sections. The first gives a scaled representation of the duration of life on this planet in comparison with the lifetime of the earth itself. The second section is an outline chronology of American history, with one column devoted to corresponding key world-developments. And the third section is a chronology of European history.

Chronological tables are as important to the historian as maps are to the geographer or a temperature chart is to the physician. They enable the historian to visualize the vast panorama of human history at one sweep. They provide an excellent means of determining time sequence, trends and developments, and the total perspective of human existence.

Time Scale for the History of the Earth

Scale: Each segment equals 100 million years

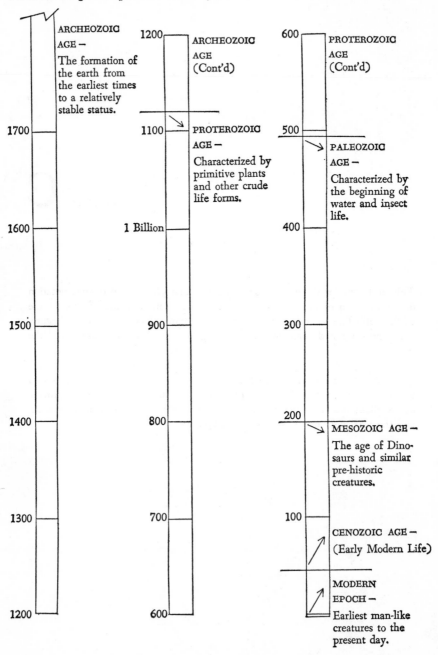

ARCHEOZOIC AGE —
The formation of the earth from the earliest times to a relatively stable status.

ARCHEOZOIC AGE (Cont'd)

PROTEROZOIC AGE —
Characterized by primitive plants and other crude life forms.

PROTEROZOIC AGE (Cont'd)

PALEOZOIC AGE —
Characterized by the beginning of water and insect life.

MESOZOIC AGE —
The age of Dinosaurs and similar pre-historic creatures.

CENOZOIC AGE —
(Early Modern Life)

MODERN EPOCH —
Earliest man-like creatures to the present day.

The period dealing with written history cannot be indicated without enlarging this scale hundreds of times.

An Outline Chronology of American History

Date	Event	Non-American
1584–1590	First English attempts at American settlement; Raleigh at Roanoke.	
1588		Defeat of the Spanish Armada.
1607	Jamestown founded—first permanent English New World settlement.	
1608	Quebec founded—first permanent French New World settlement.	
1609	Henry Hudson explores river bearing his name.	
1610	Hudson discovers Hudson's Bay; England claims region.	
1614	Dutch settle trading posts in region of New York.	
1618–1648		Thirty Years War in Europe.
1619	Meeting of first representative assembly in America—Virginia House of Burgesses; slavery introduced.	
1620	Pilgrims land at Plymouth Rock; Mayflower Compact.	
1623	New Hampshire settled. Swedes establish trading posts on the Delaware.	
1626	Dutch establish New Amsterdam (New York).	
1630	Boston settled; Massachusetts Bay Colony founded.	
1634	Maryland founded by Lord Baltimore.	
1635	Connecticut settled.	
1636	Roger Williams expelled from Massachusetts—founds Rhode Island; Harvard College founded.	
1637	Pequot Indian War.	
1638	Swedes establish a colony on the Delaware River.	
1639	The Fundamental Orders of Connecticut.	
1642–1649		England racked by civil war.
1643	Formation of the New England Confederation.	
1643–1715		Louis XIV is King of France.

Date	Event	Non-American
1649	Maryland Toleration Act	
1655	Dutch seize the Swedish colony on the Delaware.	
1662	Connecticut settlers obtain a charter.	
1663	Rhode Island and Carolina charters granted.	
1664	England captures New Amsterdam—re-names it New York; New Jersey founded.	
1673	Marquette and Joliet explore the Mississippi River.	
1675	King Philip's Indian War.	
1676	Bacon's Rebellion in Virginia.	
1680	Charleston, South Carolina, settled.	
1681	Pennsylvania founded.	
1682	La Salle journeys the length of the Mississippi River.	
1684–1688	The Dominion of New England.	
1685		Edict of Nantes.
1688		Glorious Revolution in England.
1689	King William's War.	War of the League of Augsburg.
1692	Salem witch trials.	
1693	William and Mary College founded.	
1697	Peace of Ryswick.	Peace of Ryswick
1701–1713	Queen Anne's War.	War of the Spanish Succession.
1703	Colony of Delaware established.	
1713	Treaty of Utrecht.	Treaty of Utrecht.
1729–1731	North and South Carolina established as separate colonies.	
1733	Colony of Georgia founded.	
1744	Beginning of King George's War.	War of the Austrian Succession.
1748	Treaty of Aix-la-Chapelle.	Treaty of Aix-la-Chapelle.
1754–1763	French and Indian War.	
1756–1763		Seven Years War.
1759	Battle of Quebec.	
1763	Peace of Paris, ending French and Indian War; England begins enforcement of Navigation Acts.	Peace of Paris ends Seven Years War.
1764	Passage of the Stamp Act; arbitrary beginning of the Industrial Revolution.	

Date	Event	Non-American
1765	Stamp Act Congress.	
1767	Passage of the Townshend Duties.	
1770	Boston Massacre.	
1772–1795		Poland is partitioned.
1773	Boston Tea Party.	
1774	The Intolerable Acts; First Continental Congress.	
1775	Second Continental Congress; Battles of Lexington and Concord.	
1776	Declaration of Independence; Thomas Paine writes *Common Sense*.	Watt invents steam engine.
1777	Adoption of the Articles of Confederation; Battle of Saratoga.	
1778	Treaty of Alliance with France.	France goes to war with England.
1779		Spain goes to war with England.
1780		Armed Neutrality of North; England declares war on Holland.
1781	Battle of Yorktown—defeat of Cornwallis.	
1783	End of Revolutionary War; American independence recognized.	
1786	Shay's Rebellion, *Trevett v. Weeden*; Annapolis Convention.	
1787	Constitutional Convention; passage of Northwest Ordinance.	
1789	George Washington becomes first president; first Ten Amendments; first Congress.	Beginning of the French Revolution.
1790	National debt is funded.	
1791	Establishment of First National Bank. Vermont admitted to the Union.	
1793	Eli Whitney invents cotton gin.	Reign of Terror is inaugurated.
1794	Citizen Genet Affair; Whiskey Rebellion; Pinckney's Treaty; Jay's Treaty.	
1797	John Adams becomes second president; XYZ Affair; Alien and Sedition Acts.	
1798	Kentucky-Virginia Resolutions; ratification of Eleventh Amendment.	
1799		Napoleon captures control in France.

Date	Event	Non-American
1801	John Marshall appointed Chief Justice; Midnight appointment of justices; Jefferson becomes president.	
1801–1805	Tripolitan War.	
1803	Louisiana Purchase; *Marbury v. Madison.*	
1804	Twelfth Amendment ratified.	
1805		Battles of Trafalgar & Austerlitz.
1806		Inauguration of Continental System and Orders in Council.
1807	Fulton develops his steamboat; Chesapeake Affair.	
1809	James Madison becomes president.	
1812		Napoleon invades Russia.
1812–1814	War of 1812 with England.	
1814	Treaty of Ghent ends War of 1812; Hartford Convention; Battle of New Orleans.	
1815		Battle of Waterloo; Formation of Holy Alliance.
1816	Establishment of the Second National Bank; first protective tariff passed.	
1817	James Monroe elected president; Seminole Indian War.	
1818	Great Britain and the United States agree on joint occupation of Oregon.	
1819	Adams-Onís Treaty acquires Florida from Spain.	Carlsbad Decrees in Germany.
1821	Completion of the Missouri Compromise.	
1823	Monroe Doctrine enacted to support independence in the Western hemisphere.	
1825	John Q. Adams elected president; Jackson begins the Democratic Party; Erie Canal completed.	
1828	Calhoun's "Exposition of 1828" and the "Tariff of Abominations."	
1828–1829		Russo-Turkish War.
1829	Andrew Jackson elected president—inaugurates the "spoils system."	
1830	Webster-Hayne Debates.	July Revolution in France; railroads in England.

Date	*Event*	*Non-American*
1831	Cyrus McCormick invents the reaper.	
1832	South Carolina threatens secession—nullifies tariffs of 1828 and 1832.	Reform Bill in England.
1833	Lower tariff heals rift with South Carolina; Jackson declares war on the Second National Bank.	
1835	Texas secedes from Mexico—becomes independent republic.	
1836	Tremendous western inflation and speculation; Specie Circular.	
1837	Martin Van Buren elected president; Panic of 1837.	Queen Victoria begins 64-year reign.
1840	Sub-treasury banking system set up.	
1841	William H. Harrison elected president; dies in office; John Tyler becomes first vice-president to succeed to the presidency under such circumstances.	
1842	Webster-Ashburton Treaty; Preemption Bill.	
1844	Practicality of the telegraph demonstrated.	
1845	James Polk elected president; era of Manifest Destiny begins; Texas enters the Union.	
1846	Northern boundary established at 49th parallel by treaty with England; Wilmot Proviso touches off slavery issue.	
1846–1848	The Mexican War.	
1848	Treaty of Guadalupe Hidalgo ends war; Mormans establish in Utah; Free Soil Party is formed.	Revolutions in Austria-Hungary and the Italies—France establishes Second Republic.
1849	Zachary Taylor elected president; gold rush in California.	
1850	Millard Fillmore becomes president upon death of Taylor; Compromise of 1850; Clayton-Bulwer Treaty with England.	
1852	Publication of *Uncle Tom's Cabin*; Franklin Pierce elected president.	
1853	Gadsden Purchase from Mexico.	
1854	Kansas-Nebraska Act; Perry opens Japan; Ostend Manifesto.	
1854–1856		Crimean War.
1856	Sumner-Brooks Episode; First Republican convention; "bleeding" Kansas.	

Date	Event	Non-American
1857	James Buchanan elected President; Dred Scott decision; Panic of 1857.	
1858	Lincoln-Douglas Debates.	First transatlantic cable laid.
1859	John Brown's Raid on Harpers Ferry.	Publication of Darwin's *Origin of Species*.
1860	South Carolina secedes upon Lincoln's election.	
1860–1861		Garibaldi consolidates the Italies.
1861	Lincoln takes office—ten more states secede; Fort Sumter fired upon.	Alexander II frees the Russian serfs.
1861–1865	The American Civil War.	
1862	Battle of Merrimack and Monitor.	
1863	Emancipation Proclamation; Battles of Vicksburg and Gettysburg.	
1863–1867		Maximilian is Emperor of Mexico.
1864	Sherman's March to the Sea.	
1865	Lee surrenders at Appomattox; Lincoln assassinated; Andrew Johnson becomes president; Thirteenth Amendment ratified.	
1866	Civil Rights Act passed; Freedmen's Bureau reestablished.	Austro-Prussian War.
1867	Reconstruction Act; Tenure of Office Act; Purchase of Alaska from Russia.	
1868	President Johnson impeached; Fourteenth Amendment ratified.	
1869	Ulysses S. Grant becomes president.	Suez Canal opened.
1870	Fifteenth Amendment ratified.	
1870–1871		Franco-Prussian War; Italy and Germany become united nations.
1871	Treaty of Washington with England.	
1872–1874	Major scandals of Grant regime—Whiskey Ring, Credit Mobilier, etc.	
1873	Financial panic; *Munn v. Illinois*.	
1876	Hayes elected to the presidency in disputed election; Custer's Last Stand; Bell invents telephone.	
1878	Bland-Allison Act.	
1879	Thomas Edison invents electric light.	

Date	Event	Non-American
1881	Garfield becomes president—assassinated; Chester Arthur assumes presidency; formation of the American Federation of Labor.	
1882		Formation of the Triple Alliance.
1883	Pendleton Civil Service Act passed.	
1885	Grover Cleveland first Democratic president since before the Civil War.	
1886	Haymarket Square Riot.	
1887	Interstate Commerce Act passed.	
1889	Benjamin Harrison becomes president.	
1890	Sherman Anti-trust Act; Sherman Silver Purchase Act; formation of Populist Party	
1893	Cleveland becomes president again; Panic of 1893.	
1894	Massive Pullman railroad strike broken by federal troops.	
1894–1895		Sino-Japanese War.
1897	William McKinley becomes president.	Marconi invents wireless telegraph.
1898	Spanish-American War—acquisition of the Philippines, Guam, and Puerto Rico; annexation of Hawaiian Islands.	
1899	Establishment of the Open Door policy.	Hague Conference.
1899–1902		Boer War.
1900	Boxer Rebellion.	Boxer Rebellion.
1901	McKinley assassinated—Theodore Roosevelt becomes President; Hay-Pauncefote Treaty with England.	
1902	Hay–Bunau-Varilla Treaty permits building of Panama Canal.	
1903	Alaskan Boundary dispute with England settled; Wright brothers fly airplane.	
1904–1905		Russo-Japanese War.
1906	Pure Food and Drug Act; Hepburn Act.	
1907		2nd Hague Conference; formation of Triple Entente.
1909	William Howard Taft becomes president.	
1911		Mexican Revolution; Turco-Italian War.

Date	Event	Non-American
1912	Roosevelt bolts party—forms Bull Moose Party.	
1913	Sixteenth and Seventeenth Amendments ratified; Wilson inaugurated president; Underwood-Simmons Act passed; Federal Reserve System established.	
1914	Clayton Anti-trust Act passed.	
1914–1918		World War I.
1916	Pershing Expedition into Mexico.	
1917	Purchase of Danish West Indies from Denmark; U.S. enters World War I.	
1918	Armistice ending World War I signed.	
1919	Eighteenth Amendment ratified; Versailles Treaty not ratified.	Europe signs Treaty of Versailles.
1920	Nineteenth Amendment ratified.	League of Nations established.
1921	Warren Harding becomes president; Budget and Accounting Act passed.	
1921–1922	Washington Disarmament Conference.	Anglo-Japanese Alliance terminated.
1923	Harding dies—Coolidge assumes the presidency; Gondra Treaty signed; Harding scandals begin to break.	
1924	Johnson Immigration Act establishes quota system.	Dawes Plan for reparations.
1925	Calvin Coolidge attains presidency in his own right.	
1926		British Commonwealth firmly established.
1927	Charles Lindbergh flies Atlantic; Geneva Disarmament Conference fails.	
1928	Kellogg-Briand Peace Pact negotiated.	Young Plan for reparations.
1929	Herbert Hoover inaugurated president; stock market crashes.	Tacna-Arica boundary dispute settled.
1930	Hawley-Smoot Tariff passed.	London Naval Conference.
1931–1932		Japan invades Manchuria.
1932	Reconstruction Finance Corporation established to ease depression.	

Date	Event	Non-American
1933	Franklin Roosevelt becomes president; New Deal inaugurated; Twentieth and Twenty-first Amendments ratified.	Hitler gains control of Germany.
1934	Securities Exchange Commission established; Reciprocal Trade Agreement Act passed.	
1935	Social Security Act and National Labor Relations Act passed.	Italy invades Ethiopia.
1936	Roosevelt overwhelmingly reelected.	Civil war in Spain.
1937	Roosevelt's battle with the Supreme Court.	
1938	Fair Labor Standards Act passed.	Munich pledge.
1939		Germany invades Poland; World War II begins.
1940	Roosevelt elected to a third term; Burke-Wadsworth Act establishes peacetime draft system.	Germany invades France.
1941	Lend-Lease begins; Atlantic Charter signed; Pearl Harbor attacked; U.S. enters World War II.	
1942	Naval battles of Coral Sea and Midway Island.	
1943	Teheran Conference.	Battle of Stalingrad.
1944	Roosevelt elected for fourth term; Normandy invasion; Servicemen's Readjustment Act (G.I. Bill) passed.	
1945	Yalta Conference; atomic bomb exploded; Truman assumes presidency upon the death of Roosevelt; United Nations established; World War II ends.	
1945–1946		Nuremburg War Trials.
1947	Truman Plan; Marshall Plan; Taft-Hartley Act passed.	Formation of Warsaw Alliance.
1949	Truman inaugurated president; North Atlantic Treaty Organization formed:	Communists take over China; Russia explodes atomic bomb.
1950	McCarran Internal Security Act passed; beginnings of McCarthyism.	
1951	Twenty-second Amendment ratified; Korean War begins.	
1953	Dwight Eisenhower inaugurated president; Korean War ends.	

Date	Event	Non-American
1954	Southeast Asian Treaty Organization formed; *Brown v. Board of Education* calls for desegregation.	European Defense Community established.
1955	Salk polio vaccine introduced.	
1956		Suez Canal crisis.
1957	Troops used in Little Rock desegregation.	Russia orbits first Sputnik.
1958	First American satellites orbited.	
1959		Castro takes over Cuba.
1961	John Kennedy inaugurated president; Twenty-third Amendment ratified; an American in suborbit; Peace Corps established; Bay of Pigs incident.	First cosmonaut in space.
1962	Cuban missile crisis.	China invades India.
1963	Kennedy assassinated—Johnson assumes presidency.	
1964	Enactment of War on Poverty program; Civil Rights Act passed; Twenty-fourth Amendment ratified; Gulf of Tonkin Resolution.	
1965	Lyndon Johnson inaugurated president in his own right.	
1966		France pulls out of NATO.
1967	Major riots in American cities.	
1968	Nixon elected president; Martin Luther King and Robert Kennedy assassinated.	Bombing halt over North Vietnam.

An Outline Chronology of Major European Events Beginning with the Greeks

Date	Major Events and Developments
B.C.	
2800–1200	Minoan Age in Crete.
2000	The Achaeans colonize Greece.
1600–1500	The Golden Age of Crete.
1500	The Dorian invasion of Greece.
1500–1200	The Mycenaen Age.
1000–900	Etruscans colonize Italy; the Greeks colonize the Aegean Islands; David is king of Jerusalem.
ca. 850	Homer composes the *Iliad* and the *Odyssey*.
845	Carthage founded.
800–600	Age of the Nobles in Greece.
ca. 776	First Olympic Games held.
753	Traditional date for the founding of Rome.
734	Traditional date for the founding of Syracuse.
700–600	The Greeks colonize southern Italy.
650–500	Age of the Tyrants in Greece.
621	Draco writes his Code of Laws.
594	Solon reforms the Athenian constitution.
509	Founding of the Roman republic.
493–479	The Persian Wars: Battle of Marathon (490), Thermopylae (480), and Salamis (480).
444–429	The Golden Age of Pericles—period of Athenian supremacy.
431–404	Peloponnesian Wars: Battle of Aegospotami (405).
404–371	Sparta reigns supreme among the Greek city-states.
390	The Gauls overrun the Romans.
371–362	Thebes is supreme among the Greek city-states.
338	Battle of Chaeronea won by Philip of Macedonia.
338–275	The period of Macedonian supremacy in Greece.
343–341	First Samnite War (Roman).
336–323	Age of Alexander the Great—Hellenistic Period.
326–304	Second Samnite War solidifies Roman power in southern Italy.
290	Third Samnite War ends with the Romans supreme in Italy.
264–241	First Punic War (Rome v. Carthage)—Romans gain Sicily.
218–202	Second Punic War; Hannibal crosses the Alps; Carthage becomes subservient to Rome.
215–206	First Macedonian War.
200–197	Second Macedonian War—Greeks freed from Macedonian rule.

Date	*Major Events and Developments*
171–168	Third Macedonian War.
149–146	Third Punic War—Carthage destroyed; Macedonia becomes subservient to Rome; Greeks pass under Roman rule. The Greek period ends.
58–51	Julius Caesar conquers Gaul.
44	Caesar is assassinated.
31 B.C.– 14 A.D.	Battle of Actium; Octavian rules as Caesar Augustus; the Roman Empire begins; Christ is born.
96–180	Period of the "good" emperors.
180–284	Period of general decline; emperors ruled by the army.
284–305	Diocletian is emperor—reorganizes the empire.
311	Christianity is recognized by Galerius; persecutions of Christians cease.
313	The Edict of Milan is promulgated.
323–337	Emperor Constantine reorganizes the empire; moves the capital from Rome to Constantinople (Byzantium).
325	Council of Christian churches at Nicaea.
375	Beginning of the period of barbarian invasions.
378	Battle of Adrianople—the Visigoths defeat the Romans.
379–395	Era of Theodosius the Great, the last Roman emperor to rule a united kingdom. Roman empire divides into east and west in 395. Eastern empire lasts until 1453.
410	Goths led by Alaric sack Rome.
451	Attila the Hun defeated at Châlons.
455	Vandals sack Rome after taking over North Africa.
476	Germanic leader Odoacer deposes the last Roman emperor in the west. Roman period ceases to exist in the west.
481–511	Clovis rules the Merovingian Franks—unites Europe.
493–555	Ostrogoths are supreme in Italy.
511–751	General period of decline for the Merovingians and ascendancy of the Mayors of the Palace.
527–565	Justinian rules eastern Roman empire; issues Justinian Code; conquers the Vandals and the Ostrogoths.
596	Augustine establishes Christianity among the Jutes, Saxons, and Anglos of England.
622	The Mohammedan religion is founded.
687	Battle of Testry—fragmenting Frankish kingdom is reunited.
711	Mohammedans conquer Spain after first overrunning Africa.
732	Charles Martel defeats the Mohammedans at the Battle of Tours—checks the Moorish advance.
751	Pepin creates the Carolingian kingdom.
768–814	Charlemagne rules the Franks and a united Europe; crowned emperor in 800; initiates Carolingian Renaissance.

Date	Major Events and Developments
843	Treaty of Verdun—Europe splits into the crude beginnings of France and Germany.
862	Russia is founded by the Viking, Rurik.
866	The Danes invade England.
871–900	Alfred the Great defeats the Danes and establishes the English kingdom.
936–973	Otto the Great rules Germany; the Holy Roman Empire established (962).
987	Hugh Capet inaugurates the Capetian dynasty in France.
ca. 1000	The Vikings discover North America; feudal system is at its peak in Europe.
1066	Battle of Hastings—the Norman conquest of England.
1075	Investiture struggle between Pope Gregory VII and Henry IV, the Holy Roman Emperor.
1096	Pope Urban II calls for the First Crusade.
1096–1099	The First Crusade—successfully captures Jerusalem.
1122	The Concordat of Worms temporarily solves the investiture struggle.
1147–1149	The Second Crusade—no tangible results.
1152–1190	Frederick Barbarossa is Holy Roman Emperor.
1180–1223	Philip Augustus is king of France; recovers English holdings in Normandy.
1187	Saladin captures Jerusalem.
1189–1192	The Third Crusade—results in negotiated settlement; Christians permitted access to holy places.
1190	Organization of the Teutonic Knights.
1202–1204	The Fourth Crusade—an attempt by the Italians to conquer Constantinople.
1209–1229	Period of dominance of the Albigensian heresy.
1214	Battle of Bouvines; England defeated; Frederick II rules Naples and Sicily as well as the Holy Roman Empire.
1215	King John of England signs the Magna Carta.
1226–1270	St. Louis IX rules France justly.
1228–1229	The Fifth Crusade.
1229	Establishment of the Inquisition.
1272	Edward I, king of England, conquers Wales.
1273–1291	Rudolph of the House of Hapsburg rules Germany following the Interregnum (1254–1273).
1291–1499	Swiss Confederation is developing.
1295	Marco Polo returns from his eastern travels; The English Model Parliament meets.
1297	The fall of Acre brings an end to the Age of the Crusades.
ca. 1300–1500	The period of the Renaissance.
1302	First meeting of the Estates General in France; Battle of Courtrai.

Date	Major Events and Developments
1309–1377	The Avignon Papacy (Babylonian Captivity).
1337–1453	The Hundred Years War between England and France— Battles of Crecy (1346), Poitiers (1356), and Agincourt (1415) on land, and the naval battle of Sluys (1340).
1348	Beginning of the Black Death—spreads from Italy throughout Europe.
1356	Emperor Charles IV issues the Golden Bull.
1378–1417	The Great Western Schism.
1381	Peasant's Revolt in England.
1414–1418	Council of Constance—John Huss burned at the stake for heresy (1415).
1450	Gutenberg invents printing; Jack Cade's Rebellion in England.
1453	Turks capture Constantinople—end Roman empire in the east.
1455–1485	War of the Roses in England.
1485	Battle of Bosworth Field marks the beginning of Tudor rule in England.
1492	Spain completes the Reconquista; Columbus discovers America.
1498	Vasco da Gama reaches India by sailing around Africa.
1509–1547	Reign of Henry VIII in England.
1513–1521	The Medici Pope Leo X encourages the arts.
1517	Luther begins the Protestant Reformation.
1518	Zwingli begins the Reformation in Switzerland.
1519–1522	Magellan circumnavigates the world.
1519–1556	Charles V rules Holy Roman Empire, Spain, Netherlands, and Italy.
1521	Luther condemned by the Diet of Worms.
1525	Peasant's War in Germany.
1536	John Calvin brings the Reformation to Geneva.
1540	Jesuit order founded by Ignatius of Loyola.
1542	Pope Paul III establishes the Italian inquisition.
1545–1563	Council of Trent—the Catholic Counter-Reformation.
1555	The Peace of Augsburg.
1556–1598	Age of Philip II in Spain.
1558–1603	Queen Elizabeth establishes Anglicanism in England; the age of Shakespeare.
1562–1598	Huguenot Wars in France.
1568	Revolt of the Netherlands.
1572	Battle of Lepanto—defeat for the Turks.
1588	Spanish Armada destroyed by England.
1598	Edict of Nantes issued in France.
ca. 1600	Age of Galileo, Harvey, and Kepler.
1607	English under James I found Virginia colony.
1610–1643	Louis XIII rules France with aid of Richelieu.

Date	Major Events and Developments
1611–1632	Gustavus Adolphus is king of Sweden.
1618–1648	Thirty Years War—ends with Peace of Westphalia.
1640–1688	Prussia develops under the rule of the Great Elector.
1642–1649	Civil Wars in England.
1643–1715	Louis XIV rules France—period of French splendor.
1648	Spain recognizes the independence of the Dutch Netherlands.
1653–1658	Cromwell rules England as Lord Protector.
1660	Stuart Restoration in England.
1667–1668	War of the Spanish Netherlands.
1672–1715	Peter the Great begins the westernization of Russia.
1683	John Sobieski, Polish king, halts the Turks at the gates of Vienna.
1685	Revocation of the Edict of Nantes.
1688	Glorious Revolution in England.
1689–1697	War of the League of Augsburg.
1701–1713	War of the Spanish Succession—ends with the Treaty of Utrecht.
1707	Union of England and Scotland.
1713–1740	Frederick William I establishes the Prussian army.
1715–1774	Louis XV rules France.
1740–1748	War of the Austrian Succession.
1740–1780	Maria Theresa rules Austria, Hungary, and Bohemia.
1740–1786	Frederick II expands the Prussian state.
1756–1763	The Seven Years War.
1772–1795	Partitions of Poland (1772, 1793, 1795).
1776	Watt invents steam engine; Adam Smith writes *Wealth of Nations*.
1789	French Revolution begins.
1791	Declaration of Pillnitz; French constitution completed.
1792	Monarchy abolished—France a republic.
1793	Louis XVI beheaded.
1793–1794	Reign of Terror in France.
1795–1799	Rule by the Directory in France.
1796	Napoleon begins Italian campaign—ends with Peace of Campo Formio (1797).
1797	Cisalpine Republic established by Napoleon.
1798	Battle of the Nile—Napoleon defeated.
1799	Napoleon becomes First Consul of France.
1800	Napoleon achieves major victory at Marengo.
1802	Treaty of Amiens.
1804	Napoleon made emperor of France.
1805	Nelson wins Battle of Trafalgar; Napoleon achieves most brilliant victory at Austerlitz.
1806	Confederation of the Rhine formed; Holy Roman Empire dissolved.

Date	*Major Events and Developments*
1807	Great Britain abolishes slave trade; Peace of Tilsit follows battles of Wagram and Friedland; Alexander I allies with Napoleon.
1812	Napoleon invades Russia; Spanish Penninsular War begins.
1814	Napoleon abdicates—exiled to Elba.
1815	Congress of Vienna; formation of the Holy Alliance; Battle of Waterloo.
1819	German Carlsbad Decrees attempt to stifle liberal ideas.
1821–1829	Greek wars for independence waged successfully.
1828–1829	Russo-Turkish War—ends with Treaty of Adrianople.
1830	July Revolution in France; revolutions in Poland and Italy; Belgium wins independence.
1832	Great Reform Bill passed in England.
1834	Zollverein (German Customs Union) formed.
1837–1901	Queen Victoria rules England.
1840	China opened to foreign trade.
1848	February Revolution in France; revolutions in Sardinia-Piedmont and Austria-Hungary; revolts in the Germanies.
1848–1849	Frankfort Parliament unsuccessfully attempts to unite the Germanies.
1849	Hungarian independence move, led by Kossuth, fails.
1851	Louis Napoleon becomes emperor of France.
1854	Japan opened to foreign trade.
1854–1856	Crimean War.
1858	England assumes jurisdiction over India.
1859	Austro-Sardinian War.
1860–1861	Garibaldi unites most of Italy.
1862	Bismarck assumes power in Germany.
1866	Austro-Prussian War.
1867	Political reform measures in England; Dual Monarchy established.
1869	Suez Canal opened for business.
1870–1871	Franco-Prussian War; Third French Republic proclaimed.
1871	Germany united—German Empire established.
1877–1878	Russo-Turkish War; Congress of Berlin.
1882	Triple Alliance formed; England takes Egypt.
1884	European powers partition Africa.
1891	Dual Alliance established.
1894–1895	Sino-Japanese War; Europe commences dismemberment of China.
1898	Spanish-American War.
1899	First Hague Peace Conference.
1899–1902	England engaged in Boer War.
1900	Boxer Rebellion in China.

Date	Major Events and Developments
1902	Anglo-Japanese Alliance formed; Trans-Siberian Railroad opened.
1904	Entente Cordiale formed; Russo-Japanese War.
1905–1906	First Moroccan Crisis—Algeciras Conference.
1907	2nd Hague Peace Conference.
1908	Period of the Bosnian Crisis.
1908–1909	"Young Turk" movement in Turkey.
1911	Second Moroccan Crisis; Turco-Italian War.
1912–1913	The Balkan Wars.
1914–1918	World War I: assassination of Archduke Ferdinand (1914), Battle of Jutland (1916), Russian Revolution (1917), U.S. enters war (1917), Fourteen Points (1918), Armistice signed (1918).
1919	Treaty of Versailles with Germany—treaties with Austria, Hungary, Bulgaria, and Turkey signed 1919–1920.
1920	League of Nations established.
1921–1922	Washington Disarmament Conference.
1922	Irish Free State established; Mussolini takes over Italy; World Court inaugurated.
1924	Dawes Plan for war reparations.
1925	Locarno Pact signed.
1928	Kellogg-Briand Peace Pact; Young Plan for war reparations.
1928–1932	Russia begins Five Year Plans.
1929	Worldwide depression begins.
1930	France evacuates the Rhineland.
1931	King deposed—Spain becomes a republic.
1931–1932	Japan invades Manchuria.
1933	Third Reich established by Hitler.
1935	Germany remilitarizes.
1936	Germany reoccupies the Rhineland; Italy seizes Ethiopia; Civil War begins in Spain.
1938	Munich Pact signed; Germany annexes Austria.
1939	Fascists win civil war in Spain; Germany seizes Czechoslovakia and invades Poland; Italy annexes Albania; World War II begins in Europe.
1941	Germany invades Russia; Japan attacks Pearl Harbor; United States enters conflict; Atlantic Charter signed.
1942	Naval battles of Coral Sea and Midway Island.
1942–1943	Battle for North Africa.
1943	Battle of Stalingrad; surrender of Italy.
1944	France liberated; Germany invaded.
1945	Germany surrenders; atomic bombs dropped on Japan; Yalta Conference; Japan surrenders; San Francisco Conference establishes United Nations.

Date	Major Events and Developments
1946	Fourth French Republic proclaimed.
1947	Establishment of Pakistan and India as independent countries.
1948	Israeli nation established; enactment of the Marshall Plan; Organization of American States established.
1949	North Atlantic Treaty Organization formed; Council of Europe created; Communists take over China.
1950	South Korea invaded—Korean War begins.
1951	World War II peace treaty with Japan signed.
1953	Death of Stalin.
1954	Southeast Asian Treaty Organization formed; Indochina conflict.
1955	Geneva Conference completed; Warsaw Pact signed; Bagdad Pact negotiated.
1956	Suez Canal Crisis; Hungarian Revolution.
1957	First man-made satellite (Russian) placed in orbit.
1958	Creation of the Fifth French Republic under De Gaulle.
1959	China infringes upon Indian borders as outgrowth of Tibet conflict; European Free Trade Association established.
1960	Congolese Civil War.
1961	First cosmonaut in space; Berlin Crisis.
1962	Cuban missile crisis; Russia breaks test ban.
1963	Atmospheric nuclear test ban negotiated; President Kennedy assassinated.
1964	Gulf of Tonkin Resolution.
1966	France pulls out of North Atlantic Treaty Organization.
1967	Mideast Crisis flares up.
1968	Russia invades Czechoslovakia; European monetary crisis.

3 4 5 6 7 8 9 10 11 12 13 14 15 16 17 18 19 20 21 22 23 24 25   74 73 72 71